# Tilling the Hard Soil

# Tilling the Hard Soil

Poetry, Prose and Art
by South African Writers with Disabilities

*Edited by*
*Kobus Moolman*

UNIVERSITY OF KwaZulu-Natal Press

Published in 2010 by
University of KwaZulu-Natal Press
Private Bag X01
Scottsville 3209
South Africa
E-mail: books@ukznpress.ac.za
Website: www.ukznpress.co.za

© 2010 University of KwaZulu-Natal

ISBN: 978-1-86914-190-5

All rights reserved. No part of this publication may be reproduced or transmitted in any form or by any means, electronic or mechanical, including photocopying, recording or any information storage and retrieval system without prior permission in writing from the publishers.

Cover design: Flying Ant Design
Front cover art: 'All My Father's Cattle' by Mandla Mabila
Back cover image: From 'Tilling the Hard Soil' by William Zulu

> Royalties from this book will be donated to the Open Air School in Durban. While every effort has been made to secure the signed consent of individual contributors, in a few instances this has not been possible due to changes in contact details. UKZN Press would welcome the chance to redress this.

Printed and bound by Pinetown Printers

Given back, I am less than I was, but more.
Damage is growth, restriction a freeing,
losing receiving anew: to lift up my voice,
stand at the basin, visit another city,
are not the same ordinary things
but powers and gifts.
The man returned is not the same,
and I can say, Look! having come up
I am a new man, I can choose something
new
to believe or hunt or serve.
I can begin again. *

— Lionel Abrahams (1928–2004)

\* From 'Journal of a New Man', in *Journal of a New Man* (AD Donker, 1984).

# Contents

| | |
|---|---|
| Preface | xiii |
| Acknowledgements | xix |
| Dedication | xx |
| Life after the Storm<br>   *Musa Zulu* | 1 |
| In the Beginning<br>   *Motsoakgomo 'Papi' Nkoli* | 9 |
| The Final Operation<br>   *William Zulu* | 11 |
| Please God!<br>   *Sipho Mkhize* | 18 |
| Untitled<br>   *Giulio Scapin* | 19 |
| A School for Children Like You<br>   *Mandla Mabila* | 20 |
| Jah Guide (painting)<br>   *Mandla Mabila* | 32 |
| The Dark Days<br>   *William Zulu* | 33 |

| | |
|---|---|
| K. Ward<br>*Jillian Hamilton* | 36 |
| Exploration of an Altered Self<br>*Kevin Dean Hollinshead* | 37 |
| The Operations<br>*Robert Greig* | 39 |
| Identity Scribbled in Strife<br>*Zanele Dolly Simelane* | 53 |
| On Amputation<br>*Jillian Hamilton* | 54 |
| 'shore with no feet'<br>*Kobus Moolman* | 56 |
| A New Dream Emerges<br>*Musa Zulu* | 57 |
| Tilling the Hard Soil (linocut)<br>*William Zulu* | 66 |
| Bat Magic<br>*Heinrich Wagner* | 67 |
| A Young Man Living with Epilepsy<br>*Sithembele Africa Lunguza* | 89 |
| Taking a Break<br>*Kevin Dean Hollinshead* | 94 |
| My Own Experiences<br>*Barbara Watt* | 95 |
| Three Beautiful Senses<br>*Zohra Moosa* | 99 |

| | |
|---|---:|
| When I Walk . . .  *Mak Manaka* | 101 |
| A Blind Man and his Guitar  *Mlungisi Khumalo* | 104 |
| A Quiet Time (pen and ink)  *Musa Zulu* | 106 |
| Shelter  *Kobus Moolman* | 107 |
| Somebody to Whisper  *Looks Matoto* | 116 |
| New Prison  *Sipho Mkhize* | 119 |
| In Memory of a Friend  *Piwe Mkhize* | 121 |
| Robben Island  *Giulio Scapin* | 122 |
| We are Alive  *Mak Manaka* | 123 |
| Texture of a Dream  *Motsoakgomo 'Papi' Nkoli* | 126 |
| A Poet's Life  *Piwe Mkhize* | 128 |
| Word of Mouth  *Jillian Hamilton* | 130 |
| Gazing at the Drop  *Mlungisi Khumalo* | 132 |

Limpopo Village     133
*Kobus Moolman*

Chirara     135
*Kevin Dean Hollinshead*

Taking the Wood Home (linocut)     136
*William Zulu*

A Sizzling Heart     137
*Zanele Dolly Simelane*

For the Sake of the Struggle!     139
*Sipho Mkhize*

The Apple     140
*Jacqui Edwards*

Matchgirl     141
*Shelley Barry*

Food     142
*Jacqui Edwards*

Snap     142
*Jacqui Edwards*

On My 40th     143
*Kevin Dean Hollinshead*

Reality Check     144
*Shelley Barry*

Cover Me, Cover Me     146
*Zanele Dolly Simelane*

Between These Thighs     148
*Looks Matoto*

| | |
|---|---|
| Dear Lulu | 150 |
| *Mlungisi Khumalo* | |
| A Different Corner (pen and ink) | 152 |
| *Musa Zulu* | |
| These Wheels of Steel | 153 |
| *Musa Zulu* | |
| Let Me Be Me | 155 |
| *Lungile Myeni* | |
| Self-realisation | 157 |
| *Shelley Barry* | |
| Thisability | 158 |
| *Musa Zulu* | |
| | |
| About the Editor | 162 |
| About the Contributors | 163 |
| About the Open Air School | 169 |

# Preface

What does it mean to be a disabled man or woman in South Africa today?

In a society that for several centuries has been characterised by the overwhelming practice of exclusion and discrimination, how do people with disabilities experience their own sense of difference?

And, given the recent transformation of this bitter legacy of separation and inequality in favour of inclusiveness and equality, how do people with disabilities express their new position in a changed, democratic society?

Do disabled people in South Africa, in fact, share a general reference of experience and perception that cuts across racial and economic lines, marking their allegiance to a unique and entirely contained identity?

Is it even possible to talk of 'the disabled', as if they occupied somehow a category all of their own, unmarked by cultural or social terms?

These are some of the many complex questions that a collection of this kind – in a playful yet still critical manner – seeks to provoke and challenge; while at the same time resisting the temptation to offer any quick or easy solutions. For it is perhaps the nature of all forms of social identity that they are not so much rigid definitions as fluid pathways that intersect and merge and are continually in the process of being transformed.

In this manner, then, it is of critical importance that this collection of voices by a range of disabled South Africans treats the very term 'disabled' in as broad and inclusive a manner as possible. Disability, contrary to the common perception, is not a physical descriptor only. There are a host of syndromes and traumas (psychological and otherwise) which in a clinical sense render their sufferer as 'disabled' as someone without sight or physical movement. It is fruitless then to seek after an 'authentic' or 'total' experience of disability; one that is not only representative of all forms of disability, but is also seen as being the definitive expression of it.

In fact, the term 'disabled', itself, requires from us a special degree of critical examination, lest we bandy it about too easily, as if it were not merely convenient or adequate, but actually devoid of connotation, inference and insult.

Thus, while we might readily understand a rejection of the term 'handicapped' (with its medieval sense of 'the freak'), and even see the awkward inaccuracies of the politically correct notion of being 'challenged', we are nevertheless still unable to think ourselves into a definition or description that does not automatically imply a norm or standard (as in 'abled') against which the dis-abled are set as opposite.

However important such discussions over terminology might be, we must be careful of getting bogged down in wholly academic debates that do not bring us closer to understanding or alleviating the lived reality of being disabled. In this collection, then, I have decided to follow the United Nations' Charter on Disability and use the term 'people with disabilities'; a term which has as its central motivation the desire to put the human being first and the condition of disability second.

Without sounding cynical, it has almost become a fashion now to collect, showcase and study the voices of the previously marginalised and voiceless. Thus we have women's literature, black literature, gay literature, prison writing, writing in exile (to name but a few).

This book, however, is not a showcase of the different or the exceptional. Nor is it a platform or soapbox, or any other form of public display. The authors whose work is collected here speak, I believe, on their own terms and in their own voices.

There is an inherent danger in any collection premised on the grounds of social, political or historical difference, and that is the risk of glossing over complexity and reducing all speech and action to a uniform and rigid pattern. In this collection, therefore, I have attempted to highlight the variations in experience between writers, the richness of their individual lives, in an effort to break down the monolithic category of 'the disabled' and concentrate our attention rather on the personal detail and the nuances of people with disabilities.

It must be emphasised, though, that this collection is merely a selection of material drawn from a range of types of writing, by a range of types of writers. It is inevitably, then, and unashamedly, a very personal selection. Approximately half of the authors featured might well regard themselves as writers – involved to some degree, on a more or less professional basis, with the practice of writing, while for the others the impulse simply to record their life history or share some personal insight, has been dominant.

The original idea for this collection goes back to 2002, to a conversation between Shelley Barry, who at the time worked as media manager for the Office on the Status of Disabled Persons (OSDP) in The Presidency, and Mlungisi Khumalo, who was a project manager in the same department. Some of the material was accumulated from archival files kept by the OSDP, and from organisations of people with disabilities, such as Disabled People South Africa (DPSA). Through these networks, and through the national print media, a call was also put out for writers with disabilities to submit their work to the OSDP. This part of the project was generously supported by the Flemish Government and the Department of Arts and Culture.

I also contacted the editors of literary magazines (such as Botsotso in Gauteng and Timbila in Limpopo) to elicit material from suitable contributors. Furthermore, utilising my own personal networks as both a literary editor and writer, I was able to contact several authors directly and solicit material from them.

Although all the authors were required to have some degree of 'disability' (however broadly that might be defined), I refused simply to include material on that basis alone. So, then, what general criteria did inform my choice of the material represented here?

Firstly, I looked for a degree of literariness; that is, a desire (even if only that) to use, manipulate and exploit the potentialities of written language for communication and expression. It was generally agreed by the OSDP that English (or, as I would prefer to term it, South African Englishes) would be the medium of communication. This is not a dogmatic choice, and it would be intriguing to organise future collections to include material in some of our indigenous languages.

The second criteria for selection, and one which was perhaps of greater persuasion, was the ability of authors to draw a reader into their world, and to reveal the concrete and lived experience of being disabled in South Africa today. In these terms, material that contained religious platitudes, sentimental and hollow pronouncements on the plight of the 'disabled', or that spoke in general and abstract terms of triumph and overcoming adversity, or (worse still) that depicted disability as some form of 'blessing in disguise', was rejected. I sought instead those poems, stories, scripts or snatches of memoir that opened a sensory window onto human experience, and which might have used humour, irony, outrage or even empathy to achieve this.

The third, and final, criteria was the extent to which the writing reflected what it was like living in South Africa (past or present) and was concerned with issues of significance to our society (such as Aids, imprisonment or poverty), as well as the degree to which the writing enabled the reader to experience, discover and understand more about their fellow South Africans in an intriguing and evocative manner.

The title of the collection, *Tilling the Hard Soil*, is taken from a linocut by William Zulu, who is also one of the contributors. It evokes in a powerful and succinct manner the challenges and hardships faced by people with disabilities, but, more importantly, it also describes the spirited imperative shared by every one of the writers assembled here, the impulse toward renewal and hope, toward the rich bounty of creation.

In broad terms the material within the collection is arranged in the following order: firstly, those pieces that deal with the onset of disability (whether in terms of an accident or illness) or the early childhood experiences of growing up with a disability. This is followed by a section on a particular experience common to many (if not most) people with some form of disability, and that is hospitalisation, and the dread and pain of treatment. This then leads into a short general section reflecting writers' biographical overviews of their lives, followed by material that examines a variety of social and political phenomena, such as political injustice, Aids and poverty. The penultimate part concerns two of the most ubiquitous human experiences that have obsessed writers through the ages, and which all too frequently are denied to people living with disabilities: love and sex. The collection closes with a validation that turns disability into 'thisability'.

Despite this rough structure, the material does not read like a deliberate narrative, but rather is to be enjoyed in a casual and spontaneous fashion by dipping in and out at random.

In conclusion, then, I can only wish that these stories will move and entertain you, that they will challenge your perception of disability, and that they will bring you to a new and more tolerant understanding of the complex workings of the human community.

*Kobus Moolman*
*Pietermaritzburg, February 2010*

# Acknowledgements

With grateful thanks to all the writers included in this collection, and to the University of KwaZulu-Natal Press for permission to use extracts from *The Language Of Me* by Musa Zulu, *Spring Will Come* by William Zulu and *Separating the Seas* by Kobus Moolman, and to umSinsi Press for permission to use the poem by Lungile Myeni from her collection, *Let Me Be Me*.

I am greatly indebted to Mandla Mabila for permission to reproduce his painting, 'All My Father's Cattle', on the cover of this book.

I am similarly indebted to William Zulu for permission to use the title of one of his linocuts, 'Tilling the Hard Soil', as the title of this collection.

I am grateful to Shelley Barry (formerly of the OSDP) who came up with the initial idea for this book, and to Mlungisi Khumalo and Joanna Doorasamy from the OSDP who first approached me to edit this book, and for their invaluable help in assembling some of the material represented here and also in contacting the individual contributors.

This collection was originally planned as part of an Awareness Raising Project funded by the Flemish Government and the Department of Arts and Culture, to be implemented by the OSDP in 2005. For various logistical reasons, that original plan did not come to fruition. I am enormously grateful then to the University of KwaZulu-Natal Press, and to Debra Primo, Sally Hines and especially Elana Bregin, who believed in the value of this book, and decided to push ahead with it.

This book is dedicated to all South Africans with disabilities.
Whoever you are, wherever you are, you can!

*Soli Deo Gloria!*

# Life after the Storm
*Musa Zulu*

(from *The Language Of Me*)

IT WAS RAINING HARD that evening. I still remember those heavy April rains. It was about 9.30 p.m. and I was travelling north along Umbilo Road – for what reason I can't say. The last thing I clearly recall is driving into Quentin's BP Petrol Station – whether for petrol, to pick up a cooldrink or some chewing gum, or some other purpose, I'm not sure; since I knew the attendants there, it might have been that I just wanted to share a joke with the boys. I don't remember actually buying anything or leaving the petrol station. I have tried many times to piece together what happened along Umbilo Road that evening, but there is very little that I have managed to retrieve from my memory. Whenever I reflect on those final moments, I only see flashes of bleak scenes that light up and dim away in my mind: drops of hard rain on the windscreen . . . cold showers of drizzle on my face . . . bright flashing lights. I faintly remember the commotion – someone pulling me out of the wreck, the sound of my own cries ringing inside my head. That's all. The rest is a blank. A witness from a nearby block of flats testified that she heard two loud bangs, the first like the sound of two cars colliding, then a second impact. She also claims to have seen another car in the middle of the road, but whether that car was involved in the accident, or belonged to a passerby who had stopped to help, no one can say. I have no memory of a collision, or of my car spinning out of control to smash against the brick wall in Umbilo Road; I can't recall the pain of impact, being admitted to hospital, the first days in ICU or anything else about the drama. For the next four days after the crash there was complete quiet and darkness all around me. Just quiet, not even a dream.

Then snap – I woke up! I looked around and knew instantly where I was. I could tell I was in a hospital ward by the smells – the slight odour of blood, the nauseating stench of medication and chemicals that hovered in the air of the cold room. The cold is what stands out in my memory. It was a cold not just of temperature, but of the whole environment – a chill that permeated to the core of me. I was in a room full of inert white bodies, stacked in rows of beds against the walls. I felt like I was in a Sci-Fi movie. It was early in the morning when I surfaced, around 4 a.m. and still dark. There was no one around to comfort me or answer my questions. I discovered there was a drip attached to my arm and I remember the panic I felt as I tried to lift my head but could not. Every attempt sent me spinning into blackness. The effort of moving was akin to trying to lift up the whole galaxy. It was clear that something terrible had happened to me, but what it was I could not tell. It was hard to think straight. I was still very woozy from the sedatives, drifting in and out of consciousness and reality. I felt confused, helpless, terrified and yearned for the morning light, for people, explanations, answers . . .

The sanctity of family is a critical factor in the shaping of one's personality and growth. I come from a big extended family, one of six siblings – the third-born after my twin sisters, Babongile and Bongiwe. I also have a younger brother, Thabani, who comes directly after me, followed by two small sisters, Khetiwe and Thulisile. Our house has always been full of children, not just the offspring of my mother's womb, but those of family relatives: small and grown-up, quiet and loud-spoken, lean and fat, naughty and 'every-proud-parent's-dream'. Because of the 'population explosion' at home, my world has always been made up of 'we' and 'us'. I cannot recall a time in my life when it was ever just 'me'. My background created my personality. Because I grew up in a crowd, my thoughts have always been shared. Looking back on the history of my life, I am struck by my good fortune in having the strong support networks that I have had. Whatever the experience, however challenging the road, I was never alone through any of it. There was always someone to share in the events and travel the journey with me – to stand by me, guide and advise me. I enjoy keeping close company with those who are dear to me, talking away for hours with them, sometimes deep into the night. I am simply not one for keeping my own company. The Zodiac decreed that I should be a Sagittarius, and I am the classic extrovert, comfortable in the company of others, talkative and free with my affection. I love the limelight and am never happier than when in the centre of a crowd.

I grew up closely connected with my large army of 'brothers' and 'sisters'. Back in the late 70s and early 80s, when we were still a very young crowd, all of us little ones went to church together, following each other in a line, hand in hand along the road, like baby elephants holding onto each other's tails. I don't know if this tendency was born out of fear that one of us would be suddenly snatched away or was simply a sign of our close bonding. As a family, we always had our favourite old-time stories to refer back to, remembering the standard jokes and laughing like they had just been told for the first time. We woke up together and fell asleep together, talking away nineteen to the dozen and passing coded notes to the 'trusted buddies' among us, while evading those we perceived to be the 'spies' in the ranks, or 'mother's pets'. These were the ones outside of the 'naughty' group – those whom our mother knew could always be relied on 'to tell' if an iron or a window mysteriously got broken. Like every crowd, extended families have their internal divisions, and ours was no exception. We fought at times, but on the whole we remained good friends and leaned on each other through the trying times. Together, we spent long nights concocting a golden future for ourselves, where we would live out our ambitious dreams and progress to even greater things. What we dreamed of most was shining in a crowd, winning the adoration of a multitude of fans. We fantasised about being musicians, or stand-up comedians – even generals in the army, for this would give us the chance to wear a uniform and command others. Our parents taught us to share everything, not only among ourselves, but also with others less fortunate than we were. Ours was one of the emerging black middle-class families that became evident in the townships during the early 80s. We lived in a bigger house than the average township dweller, went to better schools, and were advantaged by our better education. Yet we never thought of ourselves as being 'a cut above' the rest. Everything we had, including the special tutoring my father conducted for us, was freely shared with others in the neighbourhood. From an early age, it was instilled in me to extend the same royal treatment to everyone who enters my home, regardless of who they are; to welcome them as friends and reserve a warm space at the table of my heart for strangers as well as those well known to me. This is a philosophy that has won me many enduring friendships throughout my life.

On weekends, tennis was the big thing in our family. All of us would pile into my father's old Peugeot 404 and head off to the courts in Umlazi D Section, where the community would congregate. Regular tournaments were held there, attended by players from the adjoining Coloured and Indian communities. All of this changed in the 80s, with the institution of the Tricameral parliament, which realigned Coloureds, Indians and whites on the same side of the political fence and left blacks out in the cold. But up until that time, Umlazi, like the other townships, was a thriving centre of interactive activity, and on a weekend the tennis courts were the place to be. Those of us who could not fit into the family Peugeot would try to squeeze into one or other of my father's friends' cars. If you were unlucky enough not to get a lift, you were forced to stay at home, haunted by the walls and the loud quiet. We were not used to the experience of being alone. On one occasion, when my sister Babongile was left behind, we returned to find music blaring from the house, loud enough to lift the roof off, and Babongile looking very forlorn: 'It's very quiet here,' she complained, when asked the reason for her sad face.

We children did everything together. We all went to the same schools and had virtually the same friends. The nights were always abuzz with activity – play, song, dance . . . casino, Monopoly, cowboys, toys . . . friends. Later, in 1982, when we moved into a bigger house in the township, my father regularly gathered us all together, along with the children from neighbouring households, to give us extra lessons in English and writing. He introduced innovative ways of making the lessons easier – using word-games such as Scrabble, stories from *Reader's Digest*, and essay-writing assignments. Every outing to town – to the beachfront, Mini-Town, the countryside or Lion Park – was followed by an essay assignment which we submitted to my parents for reading and language corrections. We were encouraged to speak and write not only in English but also in isiZulu. My father's emphasis with language was always on good style, creativity and clarity of meaning. My mother still has some of those old scripts locked away in a safety box, with all their mistakes and hilarious misunderstandings.

My father, Paulus Mzomuhle Zulu, was a very well-known and respected personality in our community. He was one of the first black academics to hold a lectureship at the University of Natal, in the Department of Social Science. What characterises him best in the eyes of those who know him is his dedication to breaking down barriers through promoting the culture of respect, and his gift for making people – friends and strangers alike – feel valued and loved. Education has always been my father's crusade. He understood the importance of giving his children a headstart in life through good schooling and a good command of language. This ideal extended to the children of our township in general. In the early 80s he joined SABSWA – South African Black Social Workers' Association – running their education programme and making it a personal mission to improve literacy levels in the township and develop previously disadvantaged communities. I remember as a young boy, the many weekend trips to my father's university office, where he loved to take us. He would give us some of his books to read to keep us busy while he completed his tasks and on our way back home, would quiz us about what we'd read, always happy when we answered correctly. I grew up wanting to be like him and loved listening to him when he lectured his students.

My mother, Nkosinathi Zulu, is someone who stands tall in any crowd. She has a very commanding presence, which comes from being the firstborn in her family. She used to be a tutor at the Nursing School at McCord Hospital in Durban and is a natural teacher, with many lessons of wisdom to impart. It was my mother who taught me my love of beauty and to appreciate the gentler pleasures of life. I believe that I have inherited a big part of my personality, interests and hobbies from her. She is very creative in a hands-on way, as opposed to my father, who is creative with his head. She also draws well and is a good storyteller, spicing her tales with words aimed to stimulate the imagination of the listener. She loves looking beautiful, and holds the philosophy that if you are confident about your appearance, you will be more able to uncover the beauty and peace of mind that resides in the depths of the soul.

I love my family. They are my unit, my foundation and my strength. To me, the family is the cornerstone of a community, a society and the world. Family relations are what prepare us for the outside world – for 'the other' that we will encounter there. It's through family that we first come to know what is right and wrong, what can be achieved and by what means, and how to live through both joy and pain. This is what my family has taught me – that life can be beautiful and rich to those who work hard to earn its fruit; but that life can also be hard, and that one day everything falls to pieces and has to be picked up and rebuilt; that you have to allow for the change of those moments, and accept that there will be tears as well as laughter embodied in them. While there is a need to keep tomorrow in sight and bank for it, it is important to live as fully as you can today, for there may not be any tomorrow. It is also through my family that I have come to appreciate the importance and power of the 'Brotherhood', and to develop my respect, love and admiration for the 'Sisterhood'. It is because of the way my own sisters have conducted themselves, with dignity, humility and courage that I have learnt to value those qualities in other women and approach them from that informed perspective.

★ ★ ★

'No, you won't be able to walk again. The injuries you sustained are simply too serious for me to be able to offer any positive medical prognosis. You fractured your left clavicle, two of your floating ribs and also two vertebrae, T4 and T7. The impact created a whiplash effect which resulted in your sustaining an oedema down your spine at T6 level, and this caused instant paralysis. I'm sorry...'

The doctor went on speaking, in his unemotional, matter-of-fact voice. He was saying things about motor neurons... swollen nerves... MRI scanning... I heard the word 'wheelchair'. It all made very little sense to me – mere doctor's bullshit jargon. Every word he spoke confused and irritated me more, especially when he hinted that I might have to spend a few months in hospital. 'No ways!' was my instant reaction. I almost told him right there and then what to do with his diagnosis, but was deterred by the presence of my parents and the other elders, who were all gathered around my bed, looking very serious at the pronouncements. The mood was sombre and all the faces were wearing similar expressions, as if they were in pain – with the exception of the talkative doctor, who kept flashing his silly smiles, trying his level best to reassure everyone. I just lay there and listened, wishing he and his staff would hurry up and finish their business and leave – and take everyone else with them, so that I could be left in peace to sleep. That day went by like a lightning flash – the fastest day of my life. Many faces showed up at my bedside – family, friends, colleagues, strangers; my girlfriend was among them. But I was too tired and weak to give a damn about anything or keep tabs on who was there. Everyone was still going on about rehabilitation programmes and 'suitable institutions' when I went back to sleep . . .

# In the Beginning
*Motsoakgomo 'Papi' Nkoli*

In the beginning
Words turned into a road,
The road turned into paths,
Paths turned into streams,
Streams turned into a river,
The river turned into a road.

In the beginning
There was a road
That travelled by day and night.

The road knew no end to itself
And the road sought no end to itself.

In the beginning
We will delay your reappearance
On the plains and horizons.

In the beginning
We celebrate the ceremonies of the rebirth before the birth.

In the beginning
The crossroads give birth to never-ending.

In the beginning
We speak for a long time in silence in cryptic language.

In the beginning
Witchcraft and riddles define the beginning of all.

In the beginning
All will be done
Not knowing the end.

Forever in the beginning
The road goes on forever . . .

# The Final Operation
*William Zulu*

(from *Spring Will Come*)

IT WAS DECEMBER and the doctors had once again converged around my bed. Old man Bartfield still did most of the talking, tracing invisible lines on my X-ray with the stem of his pipe. Mr Martin and a new, rosy-cheeked doctor made occasional comments, pointing at the X-ray, while Mr Nankin consulted my bed letter. Mr Thomas stood at my shoulder, writing on his notepad and occasionally thumping me playfully on my shoulder between the sections of pelvic traction. Though I strained to grasp what they were saying I couldn't understand the medical jargon, except for a few disjointed words and phrases.

The new, stern-faced ward sister translated for me, saying that the doctors felt that it was time to operate on my back and therefore I must tell my guardian to sign the consent form. They would remove the uncomfortable pelvic traction and perform a small operation, and my problems would all be over. When I asked her for details of the operation she cut me short, saying: 'The doctors know what they are doing, William.' I watched the doctors troop off to the next bed, leaving me with many unanswered questions – questions that I now know should have been asked and answered before Uncle put his thumbprint to the consent form: What risks did the operation entail? Was there any possibility of being paralysed by it? If I was paralysed, was there any chance of correction? What about compensation in case of paralysis? But these concerns were never voiced.

That weekend, Uncle put his right thumbprint on the consent form without any further discussion or explanation as to what the operation entailed.

A day before the surgery Malume came to shave me, his plump, bearded face beaming. When I asked him my questions about the surgery, he said that he didn't know of any guarantees against or correction for paralysis. And he had never heard of anyone being compensated by the hospital in case of failure. I must not worry, however, as things would be all right. Sensing my anxiety, he joked with me, saying that I must be feeling fresh and happy without all those unnecessary hairs. Well, that was our Malume, always of good cheer.

Mama Frieda was going off duty that day but before she went she said: 'Don't worry about a thing, dear son. Trust in the doctors' expertise and God's mercy. He will truly help to guide the doctors.' Her comforting words made me relax and I had deep faith that the Good Lord would help me and keep me safe from any danger. Had He not helped me during my first operation? God would surely be on my side. Also, I had a lucky powder to lick later that night. My ancestors would also help!

Early the following morning the 'Nil per mouth' sign was hung over my bed again. I closed my eyes and opened my heart in prayer to God. 'Please dear God, let this operation be a success!' At that, deep calmness came over me and I felt that I could face anything. Later, the stretcher-bearer came to take me to theatre after an injection had been administered by the ward sister. She had patted me on the shoulder, saying: 'Don't worry William, all will be well.' At the theatre all my doctors were there and, as always, the old man was doing most of the talking. Mr Thomas playfully thumped my shoulder, winking at me as I lay on the operating table. The traction rods and rings were removed, an injection administered, and I sank into a peaceful slumber.

★ ★ ★

The Rain Prophet rose slowly to his knees, his sackcloth billowing as he knelt on the rough rock and began to pray. A song began far away and slowly grew louder until its words became clear and I could join in the singing:

> *My light will shine*
> *In my soul – it will shine*
> *In storms it will shine . . .*

Suddenly a peal of thunder rent the sky and rain began to fall in torrents. The Rain Prophet told us to hurry down the hill before the Magwetshana ('Bubbling') stream came down in full spate. We ran as fast as we could, but the stream was already swollen, rushing towards the Nsengeni River. We ran along its banks until we reached the river, its muddy waters moving sluggishly in spite of the rain. Across the water a crowd of people was shouting encouragement to us to swim across. Some of my companions were already diving into the slow-moving river, with its surprisingly warm water.

Those in front quickly reached the opposite bank and were pulled to safety. I was swimming across with the others, the people on the bank urging us on, shouting and waving. A light brown arm waved from the midst of the crowd and great joy welled within me as I recognised Mancane, my Natalspruit nurse with the honey-gold eyes. In my happiness I raised my arm to wave back, and found myself suddenly swept away by the river current. I tried to fight but was forcibly carried away towards the thundering rapids. Mancane was now running along the sandy bank, calling my name over and over, but I was powerless to save myself.

I woke up with a jolt, relieved to find that I was in a soft hospital bed. Instinctively my hand felt for the rod at the side of my scalp and the ring around my head, and I was briefly confused to find them missing. Was I still dreaming? No, I was not dreaming, the pelvic traction was gone. Joy flooded my heart and I quickly sank into a peaceful sleep where I dreamed that I was flying towards the pointed peak of Nkande hill on a powerful air current. But before I could fly over the hilltop, from where I would look down on Emondlo, I woke up to a new day in the ward. Dull pain throbbed in my pelvis and skull, and there was a new ache between my shoulderblades at the base of my neck and along the left scapula to my ribs on that side, where a slender rubber pipe was draining blood into a bottle near my bed. The relief of finding the pelvic traction removed soothed me back into another deep sleep until the following day.

★ ★ ★

The slender, hawk-nosed Mr Martin came the following morning and woke me by tickling my ear. He winked at me and a thin smile touched his mouth. He vanished behind the cradle that had been put over my bed while I was asleep. I could hear the soft rustle of my bed letter, then he suddenly threw off the blankets from the cradle to expose my feet. The ward sister watched, beaming with expectation. Mr Martin spoke softly to her and she addressed me: 'William, the doctor would like you to move your toes.' Smiling, I moved my toes. She looked at me again, saying: 'William, move your toes.' Again I moved my toes. Once more she said: 'Wiggle your toes, William,' and she wiggled her fingers to emphasise the point. Watching her eyes, I wiggled my toes. I could clearly feel them waggling to and fro. A shadow seemed to pass over the ward sister's face. She looked helplessly towards Mr Martin.

Mr Martin scratched his head, paged through the bed letter and stole a glance at me. Scratching his nose, he took off the blankets from the cradle, asked for a pin and pricked my feet and my leg asking: 'Can you feel this?' I looked dumbly at him and the sister echoed his question. 'Can you feel the pricks, William?' I shook my head. The doctor and sister removed the blankets and the cradle, lifted my feet from the bed and carefully put them on the floor. Pain shot through my side as I was lifted to a standing position. My senseless feet folded under me and I would have crashed to the floor had not Mr Martin pushed me backwards against the bed. They lifted me back onto the bed and hastily covered me. Mr Martin wrote on my bed letter, took out his handkerchief and wiped his perspiring hands and face. He mumbled something to the ward sister, then walked away forever, never to come near my bedside again.

It did not take long for me to realise that I was paralysed from the chest downwards. All sensation was gone except in the region between my shoulders and upwards from there. Later, I would come to know that the operation had begun at the base of my neck and cut below the left scapula to my left side. In the second week, the ward sister removed the sutures on my pelvis and took out the drainage pipe from my side. She tried to console me, saying: 'Don't panic William. In this type of operation sensation takes longer to come back. So don't worry, all will be well, take my word for it. Six weeks,' she said, raising her thumb. I accepted what she said and held onto it with all my heart. I also trusted in the support of my God to help bring back sensation and let me walk again.

When Mama Frieda came back on duty the following week, she was stunned to know that I was paralysed. She comforted me in her soft voice, saying: 'Ngoanaka, there is hope that you are going to be all right, but it will take time.' She tried to cheer my doubting heart with presents and delicacies. As I couldn't turn on my own, Mama Frieda and Malume came to turn me onto my sides, back and front and clean and change my soiled linen. Sometimes Mama Frieda would come to empty the urine bag or change the catheter. I was still convinced that I could waggle my toes, but I was to learn later that it was all in my mind – a phantom feeling. Sometimes my feet would jerk and I would think that movement was coming back, but I learnt to recognise that these were only muscle spasms. Above all, I held tight to the ward sister's promise that all would be well in six weeks.

I would think with trepidation of Uncle, who had gone home for the December holidays. The last time he had visited me was when he put his thumbprint onto the consent form. He had reminded me to lick the lucky powder and had given me R10, some Coke and fruit. I remembered how, before he left, he had taken my hand in his stubby, calloused one, gazed into my eyes and said: 'Let you be well young man. Let our ancestors be with you.' I had told him to pass on my regards to all at home in Natal and tell them that I would soon be well and home again. I could see that Uncle was looking forward to his holiday at home with his growing family and many friends. There would be feasting, traditional beer, singing and dancing. I had watched his light step as he walked away from my bed and imagined the look of gladness on his face when he found me cured. But things had drastically changed since then, and my heart bled as I thought of his distress when he found out I was paralysed.

When he paid me a visit early the following January, he found me flat on my stomach reading a book, a bed cradle covering my legs and hips, keeping the bedclothes from touching the wounds. His greetings brought me swiftly back to the real world and we shook hands. When he asked me about my health, I said a silent prayer before telling him the truth about my situation. I heard myself telling him that since the operation that was to cure me I had become a completely changed person. I was paralysed from the chest downwards. Then I added hastily: 'The doctors have promised that all will be well within six weeks.'

I watched him taking it all in, his face visibly blanching as he reeled in shock at my words. We couldn't talk after that, for there was nothing to be said, only tears to be shed.

Days became weeks and weeks became months but nothing changed for better, only worse. Pressure sores developed on my hips and buttocks. Hope painfully dwindled and my prayers faltered, stopped and died. There was no need to pray for there was no God to hear my prayers. Even if He heard, He had shown His true colours as an uncaring God! What if I had been deluding myself all these years believing there was a God? There was no God, no Bible, no truth, only lies, lies, lies!

I was grown up enough to think for myself; therefore, from that time forth, I would allow no one to tell me anything about God and faith in His love. Life had lost its meaning and promise, and I sank into the oblivion of my sad thoughts. I lost all interest in others near me, including Mama Frieda. She was kind but could not help me in my dilemma – she could not bring back my sensation, my mobility, my life. I thought of many ways to end my life and be free from this hardship – this torment of soul. If I could have had the chance, I would gladly have killed myself, and I didn't care whether I went to Hell for it – if Hell even existed – because I was already in Hell! I hated God with all my heart and mocked anyone who dared to mention the word God to me.

I was only eighteen years old.

# Please God!
## *Sipho Mkhize*

Oh! God, my God! I remember the year 1973;
On October 10 the baby was named Sipho;
Please God, tell me what was that gift for?
Was it a gift for suffering or oppression?
God! Now I'm a square peg in a round hole;
Where I stay there's no mother no father,
I celebrate my birthday with tears.

My God, before I sleep I do the Roman Cross;
The Roman Cross as a road leading me to the bright
Future.
    Please God! bring love, joy and peace to me.

# Untitled

*Giulio Scapin*

What would I have been
by now
if I was
an able-bodied person?
Maybe a doctor
or a lawyer!
Even a builder!
But now
I'm only
a disabled
person.

# A School for Children Like You
## *Mandla Mabila*

MY GRANDMOTHER NEVER forgot to tell and re-tell the stories of how my disability came about. Most of the stories conflicted with the way the doctors explained the cause of my disability, but she had one favourite story and it has become my favourite story too. It has to do with the wind. Apparently on one fine afternoon the wind rose up unexpectedly and encircled me, almost lifting me up to the clear blue skies where pieces of paper and other debris were flying around. Seeing the impending danger my grandmother threw herself on me and shielded me from the wind, until the wind 'decided' to leave me alone and died down. The following day I started getting sick. It started off like flu and became more and more serious, until my family was forced to take me to a hospital in Nelspruit. This was the beginning of a period of hospitalisation for me that lasted for many years to come.

There were always two explanations of my disability at home; one of course was polio (the Western medical term for my condition), which is really not the 'real' explanation as far as my family is concerned. The 'real' explanation has to do with the wind to some extent; in other words, with witchcraft. I will not go into whether these stories are true or not because it seems to me that is not the point. After I had been to prophets, or spiritual healers, and traditional healers and nothing much had changed, my family must have given in to the idea of my going to hospital. The contradiction here was the fact that my family, being staunch Christians, could not be seen to believe in witchcraft and other such things, according to the Bible, which was the backbone of our church and family.

I only remember coming back from the hospital in Nelspruit, where I had spent years being examined by doctors after it was discovered that I had polio. I must have been about seven by then, having contracted polio four years earlier. There were, and still are, no memories of the hospital, the operations or anything else to do with the hospital for that matter. But I had brought home with me the smell of the hospital. I lay on the big bed in the kitchen, while the rest of my family, like the doctors at the hospital, inspected me, their faces growing bigger as they bent over to either kiss or take a closer look at me. Of great interest to them were the operations on both my ankles; the rest of me did not seem to matter much at the time. The expressions of disappointment, joy and, sometimes, anger were written all over their faces.

My family seemed to have expected some change somewhere in my body when I was discharged from hospital; the change apparently had not taken place or had done so to an unsatisfactory extent. I only recognised my grandmother, while everybody else seemed to fade into the dark background of our small kitchen, which was almost always covered with smoke, soot and the smell of delicious bean soup on the black coal stove. My grandmother is difficult to forget because of her radiant beauty, her intelligence and strict discipline, which she tried with little success to instil in us. I felt very small lying on that double bed and even smaller with my grandfather standing near the bed; he is still a giant. He is a quiet, kind giant, but also a strict disciplinarian. After a week or so I settled in at home and my family began to look ordinary again.

The time came to make new friends and I made as many of them as I made wire-cars. These were the days when making friends was the most natural and easiest thing to do. For us children, family standing was measured only in relation to the number of toys one had to play with.

Adults made an issue of children's home backgrounds. Sometimes they examined the toys we played with to see which were more expensive. We children became even more convinced that adults were not bright at all. Mothers would always ask where your father worked; no, first they asked you if you had a father to start with. I grew up being told that I had no father. Nothing happened to him, I just never had one. So those women who always asked about our fathers got that explanation, after which they looked at me funnily, as if something was missing in my head. I had so many friends, who needed a father? So I never asked about him or what happened to him. Nothing was ever explained to me except that he was alive and well-to-do in Swaziland. In my mind my father was a big, dark, gray shadow cast in the opposite direction from mine.

New Clare was one of the smallest, but also the busiest, townships in Barberton (second only to White City). New Clare was where my grandparents' house and my first home was. It was a three-roomed house with nine people living in it. All the houses in New Clare back then were three-roomed. They were in one of three pale, chalky colours: blue, pink or yellow. The paint would come off like chalk if you leaned against the wall. In the sitting room there was a double bed where my mother and, sometimes, my uncle slept. I slept on the floor under the dining table that always seemed so big and out of place in the sitting room. My four aunts slept in the kitchen on the floor, and on the old double bed whose four legs were balanced on used two-litre paint tins that were filled with sand up to their brim, so the bed was quite high. It was not long before, for some unknown reason, I was transferred to the kitchen; the double bed had been moved out of the kitchen by then and a big white table had taken its place. I was to sleep under the new table for a few years to come, and this became my favourite spot.

The reason I did not share a blanket with one of my aunts who also slept on the floor was that I had a problem, if you can call it that. Every night I had this dream: that my friends and I were jumping into warm puddles. And hence my blankets had a thick smell of urine every day, since my mother only washed them after a week or so. By the time my blankets were washed the smell would almost have reached a solid state, quite thick. To embarrass me further, my mother took them out in front of my friends, especially girls, who knew who the blankets belonged to. The blankets were hung on the washing line outside every morning to be dried by the sun.

The hiding I received on a daily basis to make me stop my peeing 'habit' did not seem to be of any help at all. There were, however, two good things about the intoxicating stench of my blankets. Firstly, I never had a problem with mosquitoes; everybody else did. Secondly, every time I smelt my blankets I fell asleep . . . they had a drugging effect; and I didn't need any lullaby either. I had this particular dream until I was twelve and in boarding school.

The only bedroom in the house belonged, like all of us and everything else in the house, to my grandparents. That bedroom was a 'no-man's-land'. Another no-man's-land was our toilet, a tiny room a few metres behind the house. In the toilet was a black bucket on which we perched to 'do our business'. The buckets were emptied twice a week by 'faceless' men, who seemed nothing short of zombies to us children. They didn't even have names. Rumour had it that one of these men was Muzi's father, but he denied it every time we asked him about it. Muzi was one of my many friends and he loved eating; anything at all, he ate it. He loved boxing as well, something we had in common, except that I loved watching it and he preferred participation in the sport. On days when he was itching for a fight even a simple 'hello Muzi' could spark fury and, of course, a fight. He was great. There was a Zulu song called '*Thathela mfana*' – 'Hurry up boy' – which, if sung out loudly enough, offended the bucket-emptying men for some unknown reason. So if you sang it and they heard you, they would come and empty the contents of three days' worth of toilet bucket on your doorstep.

The toilet was my favourite place; during the day, that is, because I used to spend about an hour or more in it, singing. The toilet walls had a way of amplifying my voice, making it sound big. I liked that. My mother's constant compliments, such as, 'This boy is going to be a good singer one day, I'm telling you', went a long way as well. I found out early in my life, though, that I was not cut out for a singing career; maybe an instrument, but not the voice.

The rainy summer season made me miserable beyond redemption, because the only way I moved around (other than being carried by somebody) was to pull myself along the ground and all over the kitchen floor, where I was between people's legs and in the way. So after the rains, when the ground was wet, I was not allowed to go outside where all my friends were running around and jumping into dirty puddles. Instead I was subjected to hopelessly boring and frankly stupid adult conversations inside the house. 'This is child abuse,' I used to think to myself. After it rained I would have to be carried out to the toilet, and this meant that I couldn't go there for recreational purposes such as singing. What was worse was that it took days before the ground was completely dry again, and I was forced to stay indoors in the meantime. I hated being indoors. The saying, 'all work and no play makes Jack a dull boy' made a lot of sense to us children. If we had our way we would only use two hours out of the twenty-four to sleep; the rest would be used for something too sophisticated for the adult species to enjoy . . . play. I made so many friends that my grandparents' house was transformed into a kindergarten after school and on weekends.

I was not attending school then; my mother said something about a principal refusing to admit me to his school because his staff wouldn't know how to deal with me. He also said I would slow down the progress of the rest of the class. I viewed this as just some of the stupid things adults talked about, and in any case who needs school when you have hundreds of friends to play with? I had seen my three aunts and uncle go to school. They didn't seem terribly excited about going there. They were bullied by my grandmother to go every morning, so I concluded that school couldn't be much fun. Most of my friends went to school and said that they hated it. These were the times of corporal punishment in many schools. I remember overhearing my grandmother swearing by her own grandmother that she would never take her children to lenient teachers because 'the children don't learn anything from a teacher like that'. Beating children up was in style back then. My aunts would sometimes come back from school and show off the marks left by the teacher's cane. All of this didn't serve as incentive for me to go to school, so when the principal refused to admit me to 'his' school I thought he was the coolest principal ever.

Playing back then was an uncomplicated affair and was definitely more fun. We didn't have to buy toys because the money was never there in the first place and because virtually anything could be turned into a toy. Bricks were used to make buses and old pantyhose were used to make tennis balls. I especially liked bricks because they could be used as weapons when and if the need arose, which was often enough. I was lucky because now and again I would get a proper toy from my grandmother's employers; usually it would be an old metal toy car with only one wheel left, and I would make my own wheels from a broomstick, which I sliced into the same thickness, making a hole in the centre. There were also hundreds of games to choose from. The only important thing among children then was one's willingness to play, and it did not matter who you were or where you came from; we were all children and children play together.

Playing was probably the most healing exercise I could ever have participated in as a disabled child. The field of play was uninhibited for all of us. This was where we could say what we really thought and felt. With hindsight, playing must have been for me not only an integrative tool to the larger society, but also a way for me to engage society. Playing was also a good equaliser because all of us could play and nobody played better than others, unless of course in sport.

As mentioned before, I got around by pulling myself along the ground and, somehow, I had an elegant and dignified way of doing it, especially when I went to impress girls with my good looks. Pulling myself along the ground was to me what walking is to the able-bodied, and certainly my friends and family didn't make me feel that there was any difference. I knew I couldn't do some things like stand up or run but that didn't constitute disability to me; not like the guy I knew who was always on his mother's or somebody else's back. Now *he* was disabled. I was also carried around sometimes on my mother's or aunt's back, and every time I saw that poor boy on his mother's back my heart went out to him. My family expected me to do my chores like everyone, but they were not the 'manly' ones like cutting wood for the stove or slaughtering a goat on Christmas Eve, so I always felt like I was missing out. Of course I never really found out what exactly I was missing out on. Among other things my chores included wiping and packing the plates and pots away. My grandmother was always happy with my work, not because it was excellent but because I had done it. The sense of belonging was very strong and reassuring.

One of the many games we children played was something called '*mashayelana*'. This was a game of penalty shootouts without the actual game of soccer. I would sit on the ground facing my opponent and all we did was kick the ball between us with the aim of scoring more goals. Sometimes my opponents would make obviously stupid mistakes and lose matches, after they had already won the first six or ten matches. These 'stupid mistakes' were not as obviously stupid to me back then, though.

As I sat on the ground I would kick the ball, or rather the ball would bounce off my foot; to ensure that my shot was big enough to score, my opponent would have to kick the ball very hard, so that it ricocheted back to him with enough speed to go through his legs. Basically, I won games through a lot of 'own goals' by my opponents. Sometimes I would be used as a goalkeeper for some of the more serious soccer matches on the calendar. My success as a goalkeeper depended on a number of things. Firstly, the ball had to move along the ground; secondly, my goal posts had to be narrower than usual, to the irritation of our opponents; and thirdly, no hard kicking of the ball was allowed so as to make it easier for me to make 'great' saves.

The opponents' goal posts would usually be the toilet and a brick; they were also supposed to be three times as wide as mine. My goal posts were usually my grandfather's old boot and the peach tree. So I just sat between the goal posts and pretended I was Peter Barluck, Kaizer Chief's goalkeeper and in my opinion the best in the world. Banda of Orlando Pirates was nothing by comparison; most of my friends thought so too.

The best time in the world was when we were up to mischief. I would borrow the trolley that my grandfather had stolen from the mine where he was working; it was used for carrying bags of asbestos. It also carried me. My friend S'fiso was never too tired to push me around the whole township on that trolley. I would repay him by humming the sound of a Datsun Nissan engine for several kilometres on end. On that trolley we were ready to conquer the world. Barberton was, and still is, strongly divided along racial lines. It has always been that way, with the black townships first; the Coloured township next; followed by the Indian township; after which one arrived at the whites-only suburbs. Physical barriers like the railway line and the main road divided these areas and you did not cross over to the other side; it was supposed to be 'suicidal'. It was not long before S'fiso and I started enjoying the sense of danger and excitement in crossing the line and being chased by the Coloured boys. We sneaked into the Coloured township stadium, which at least had good grass to sit and play on. Blacks were barred from these grounds.

S'fiso and I showed up at the stadium and the Coloured boys gave chase as soon as they saw us, and so we ran for dear life, adrenaline pumping. S'fiso would rather we got caught than leave me behind; no matter what, he ran with me on the trolley. What I could not work out was whether S'fiso never abandoned me because he loved me so much or because generally, when he was caught with me we were not punished – either way he was my best friend. When we were caught our captors would often say that because of me they would not harm us. I just thought I was a lucky guy. Even back home I would be protected by my family from talk of me being part of the notorious group of boys who stole vegetables from the nearby school garden. My family's argument was always that 'he wouldn't harm a fly'. What my family didn't know was that I was second in command of that group and that harming flies was a waste of time for us; we killed people's chickens and pigeons with slingshots that we made with our own hands – I was very proud of that. If it was a serious 'crime' that we had committed, either my grandmother or mother would give me a beating and the scolding would last for a month; my grandfather would just punish and that was the end; he was great.

The trolley took me to the movies as well. Makhoba's store was the most successful and, arguably, the biggest general store in the township. It was situated about 300 metres from our house. Sitting under the peach tree, I could see the people going in and out of the store. Some went in to actually buy a few things, but the boys and girls went there to check each other out, while their parents sat waiting for their goods back home. Older boys gathered on the stoep of the store to gamble; either 'five cards' or 'dice'. The store was an exciting place, filled with noise; the smell of greasy 'vetkoeks' and 'mango atcha' dominated. If you were serious about being married one day, you stood at shop verandas. On occasion the owner's children would organise movies, which were screened on the outside wall of the store facing the dirt road, and these were a big attraction. These movies would be screened perhaps twice a year if we were lucky; we were doubly lucky, because the viewing was free of charge as well. The only challenge was securing a place to sit on the densely populated ground. In summer it was a pleasure to go to these movies because the evenings are warm in Barberton and there's more grass to sit on, as opposed to winter evenings when we sat on the cold, dry sand. The only problem in summer was that it rained a lot, and that meant no movies. It was during the movie times that I went closer to the store and became part of the festivities around the store that I otherwise only looked on from afar. I just hopped on the trolley and off we went to the movies . . . *Tarzan the King of the Apes* was showing on one occasion. Strange guy, this Tarzan. In my community, if a baboon was seen in your yard or your house you would be dubbed a witch. Tarzan was brought up by the apes, so we wondered about him.

Movies were big but an even bigger event in the children's calendar took place once every year. Our parents struggled to get us to sleep on the eve of this particular event. It happened about two weeks before Christmas. The government of the day (I think the Prime Minister was called Vorster, or something like that) used to give out presents to the black children of all the townships of Barberton. On this day, not only did we get presents, we also got to see white people in the flesh and they were a rare sight, especially for children. Adults like my grandmother who was a domestic worker saw them almost every day. The only white people I had seen were the doctors at the hospital and the police who came to look for the man who lived next door, something to do with dagga. This was the time of the year when beliefs about whites were reinforced in our township among adults and children alike. We would be woken up early in the morning, around six, to bath and be scrubbed clean with a rough stone that was used especially for scrubbing dirt off somebody's back. The scrubbing was usually a particularly painful experience, but on this day we even asked our mothers to scrub us, much to their delight at the opportunity to inflict pain.

We would even get to wear our Sunday clothes, and then run like hell to the hall where the festivities were taking place. The queue to the hall would be a few hundred metres long, filled with children of all ages. Once I saw three grown-up boys with a lot of beard standing in the line. They were not supposed to be there and were duly kicked out. Average children would spend half the day in the line, while 'tsotsis' or 'clevers' like us made our way to the front in a flash. A 'tsotsi', roughly translated, means a thug or gangster. So calling a boy a 'tsotsi' was actually a compliment. As soon as people in the line saw the trolley they would say, 'Agh, shame!' And then usher us to the front of the line. We would receive our goodies that we had waited the whole year for: a half-litre bottle of Fanta Grape, Seven-Up or Coca-Cola; two buns; and a packet of sweets. The adults would be just as delighted as the children when we got home with these goodies.

We would drink the Coca-Cola for about two hours until everybody had finished. This was the only time in the year that many children (certainly, us) got the chance to have some real cooldrink, as opposed to Cool-Aid the whole time. Cool-Aid was an artificial soft drink in powder form. One would just add water and sugar and then enjoy. I did not like Cool-Aid, mainly because we had too much of it and because it didn't have bubbles. On top of this, after drinking it my lips would be stained red or whatever the colour flavour of my Cool-Aid was. So when I went out to play my friends would say, 'You had some Cool-Aid today', and I wouldn't ask them how they knew.

Near my grandparents' house was a huge, grey building made of concrete. We called it '*ebhavu*', something I can't find an equivalent for in English without losing the meaning of the word. '*Libhavhu*' literally means bathtub or a washing basin; the place was full of washing basins and liveliness. What this building really was, was a meeting place for all kinds of people from different townships. There were showers and two bathtubs for women; three showers for men; bucket toilets for men and women (in separate areas, of course), and a large area with at least twenty washing and rinsing basins, all made of concrete. The building was often buzzing with excitement, especially after school and after work. The buzz would continue right into the night, with people taking showers, doing their washing, exchanging gossip, smoking dagga or having sex. There were no doors to this building, except in the toilets; the shower areas had no roofs either. Old men like my grandfather showered there in the open and watched the sky while they showered. They would always try to chase the children away, but only succeeded in making the children more interested in peeping. I took my shower there as well. I moved myself along the ground to get there, but on my way back from the shower I would be more dirty than before. The building was destroyed in the 1985–86 period – something to do with racism and apartheid, the adults said. It used to be a meeting place for our group and a place to meet our girlfriends; hence the adults didn't want us going there unsupervised. The place was cleaned and maintained by an old man – we called him 'Mr Bucket' because he carried one every day. These are just a few among the thousands of other exciting moments of growing up in Barberton.

'Jah Guide' – Mandla Mabila

# The Dark Days
*William Zulu*

(from *Spring Will Come*)

ON THE WEEKEND Uncle Vukudle paid me a visit. He had brought an unexpected visitor with him – my mother. The sight of her was not altogether welcome to me. I felt initially very distant from her and filled with reproach towards her. Since my operation, much had changed in me and my outlook on life had altered considerably. I had come to feel that my illness and subsequent paralysis was God's retribution for the sins of my parents, and I held my mother personally responsible for my suffering. Nonetheless I recognised that she had travelled a long way to visit me, so I kept my thoughts to myself. She hugged me, kissed both my cheeks and gazed deep into my eyes for a long time. Her own eyes brimming with tears, she asked if she could look at me. When I nodded, she drew back the coverings from the bed cradle that covered me. I was lying flat on my stomach and could not see her expression as she gazed at the long scar running down my spine and along the left scapula. She looked down to my thin, wasted legs, slowly lifted the gauze and saw the gaping wounds on my hips. All this time Uncle was as still as a statue, only his eyes and agitated hands betraying his emotions.

It had been a long time since my mother had last seen me, before the start of my long journey in search of a cure. Strangely, I did not hold her absence against her, for I realised that she had her own burdens to carry.

She had to look after her growing family in the absence of my stepfather, who spent most of his time away working in Durban, only managing to come home during the Easter and December holidays. She had to raise four children on the meagre money he sent. Despite my inner conflicts, I had no wish to hurt her and after my initial reaction was, in fact, happy to see her there at my bedside. I did my best to cheer her up by telling her about Mama Frieda and showing her the food that Mama had given me.

My mother said a moving prayer, pleading with her God to heal me. I found her prayer a waste of emotion but I didn't tell her so. She gave me two lumps of sweet potato, which she broke and fed to me as if I was a small child. She could not understand that inside, I was an old man, grown up by my experiences in the hospital. I told her and Uncle of the operation that would help to heal my sores. Uncle consulted with mother who agreed that he should sign the consent form. She encouraged me to have faith in the Lord, who would help this doctor with his operation. Again I couldn't hurt her feelings, and said I would trust Him. Uncle went to the ward sister to sign the consent, leaving me to make small talk with my mother, with whom I found I had little to say. Before leaving, Uncle gave me some money and then departed with a handshake. My mother kissed me again, and they left. I watched them weaving their way through the other visitors until they vanished around the corner of the ward. The only tangible proof that my mother had been with me was the lump of cold sweet potato in my locker.

For weeks after her visit my thoughts would constantly be at Emondlo, far, far away. I felt a deep yearning to get out of the hospital, but this quickly died as I thought of my physical situation, my helpless condition, with only my torso and head functioning. It had not yet dawned on me that I was to survive the rest of my life this way, by the strength of my arms, the steadfastness of my mind and the dreams of my heart.

Since Uncle had signed the form, Mr Maxwell proceeded with the operation on my sores. We had agreed on 'local anaesthesia', which would enable me to remain conscious through the procedure, for I had a deep fear that I might not wake up from the operating table. But when I saw the blood, I fainted, so he was obliged to put me fully under. I came to on my bed when it was all over, lying flat on my stomach. Days later when Mr Maxwell came to see me, he patted me on the shoulder and told me that I would be up and about soon. Although I was sceptical I hoped he was telling me the truth. I began to imagine myself sitting up and playing games with the other boys again. In the meantime I had to stay in bed and the physiotherapist came to exercise me.

Many nights after lights out, I would draw the sheet over my head and in the inky blackness, let my mind escape from the ward and travel freely on the long journey home. I would take a taxi to Katlehong, from where I would take a Valiant (nicknamed 'Valaza') all the way to Emondlo. I imagined myself walking – never in a wheelchair – up and down the home streets, looking up my friends and former playmates. But since I could not conjure any dialogue between us, I would give up the fantasy in frustration and return to the reality that I was stuck in my hospital bed with an uncertain future ahead of me.

# K. Ward
## *Jillian Hamilton*

down at the end
of the corridor
a baby frets
cat-sounding

my head aches
thought-dulling

in the room next door
a man coughs
so deep
and so long
that i fear his lungs will end up
splattered
all over the clean
green
walls

black-glistening
pus-slithering-sliming
tobacco-smelling

# Exploration of an Altered Self
## Kevin Dean Hollinshead

(for Cathy Hanauer)

Can we see what is wrong
With this patient?
Blood and bones in disarray
Mangled fibula, tibia
Abrasions, an ugly sight.
Stitches, pins and pills will do
To take away that pain inside
Come back when you are well
For I cannot deal with that which you hide.
Science is my game
Study the man from the outside in
And tell him how to feel
Dare I place myself in your position?
And see the world as you do
Dare I try to understand?
The catastrophic effect
Of a single careless moment
Upon a carefree life.

Dare I ask how you feel
When I know your answer
Will not be what I want to hear?
Don't tell me about your pain
It takes time to heal.

# The Operations
*Robert Greig*

FIRST WAS THE BABIES' ward, then the girls', then at the end the boys'. The roof was curved, high and dim. Once, in the boys' ward, we heard the babies begin to cry, great wails curling, ascending. A pigeon, trapped, flew above with a clap and clatter of beating wings. Then the girls, afflicted by the sound of the bird, began to cry. We did not cry but hid our heads beneath the pillows, fearing for our eyes. The braver ones threw pillows till the nurses rushed in, agitated in Afrikaans, complaining, their arms waving inadequately.

One night, John, who usually wore thick black spectacles and was thin, came back from his op. (My father always called operations, jauntily, ops, so I did too.) He had had a foot cut off and his return ushered a miasma of morphine. He looked blind without his spectacles. They rolled John's trolley in squeakily from the operating theatre. The sour anaesthetic surrounded him: his bed was mounded, as if they had left the leg there to swell and balloon. That night, he began screaming. His eyes were shut but he screamed in sleep or drugged delirium. Nurses in white uniforms and brown stockings flocked around him, the curtains on rails scraping harshly. Their arms dived beneath blankets, they looked abstractedly at us and they gave him injections to propel him beneath the turbulent pain. We felt sorry for him. The noise dwindled in a drizzle of cries; we slept.

Four hours later, his screams leaked then flooded again, insinuating themselves into our sleep, prising us up and out into the ward's grainy dawn light. The nurses returned and fussed with blankets and spoke soothingly but they did not inject him again: no doctor was there to authorise it.

'We can't sleep,' someone complained. 'Try,' Nurse Viljoen said curtly. Her white uniform stretched tight across her elephantine bum. I'd bet her a Coke I would be out of the hospital in six days. She said she knew better: I'd be there for two weeks.

John cried and he yelled. A boy whose bed was beside his bashed the iron pillars of John's bed. 'Shut up, you,' he said angrily. John was still writhing in coiled fumes of anaesthetic. The boy on the other side also hit the steel rails of John's cage, with its giant blankets mounding where his leg had been and where now we imagined was a gasping crimson gap. What did they do with the severed arms and legs? Someone said they put them in the fire. We sat silently, imagining arms and legs laid like logs upon the flames and hissing. The boys banged and banged; the metallic clank in my ears as I tried to sleep, my head below the blankets to keep out screams and dangerous clattering wings above.

The next morning, he was moaning, softly, slowly and rhythmically: 'Ooooh, ooooh.' Someone imitated him and we giggled. He was ashen and though his eyes were open he did not seem able to see us. All he had was pain, all round him, nesting upon his face.

The nurse came in to prep me for my operation. 'Will it hurt?' I asked, hoping for comfort. She had very blue eyes and she looked at me calmly.

'If you cut yourself, it hurts?' she asked.

'Yes.'

'Well, they're going to cut you with big knives,' she said unemotionally. I hoped I would not moan like John. I hoped the other boys would not bang my bed. I hoped they would not cut my feet off by mistake and feed them irretrievably to the flames. I didn't want to be like Douglas Bader in a camp where the Germans took his feet away and he could not walk on toe-less stumps. I hoped I would awaken again, even sick and crying, just wake.

She drew back the blankets, a pail of silver glinting instruments beside her. She checked a sheet of paper attached to my bed. 'You're going to have plaster up to your waist,' she said. 'Take off your pyjama bottoms.' I slipped out; she drew the curtain round my bed. She soaped my legs and began shaving the hair off – the new male brown hair I was proud of. The water was warm and soft, and then it cooled. I lay looking at the curved high ceiling, pretending to be somewhere else. Then she plucked my penis and shaved around it and between my thighs. I concentrated on keeping it soft, athwart my thigh, not looking down, caught between embarrassments and prickling stiff pleasure. She did not meet my eyes. I thought of school.

'That's it,' she said. 'Sleep well.'

My penis and balls looked like the shrivelled gizzards of a plucked mauve chicken. I was hungry but they would not give me anything to drink or eat; it would make me sick after the anaesthetic. I lay all day, watching the light change in the ward, keeping still, so fear would not notice and pounce. Then a nurse came with an injection. I did not look. Its slide into me stung. The boys on each side did not talk to me. I wanted to sleep but visitors started arriving with cheery voices and plastic bags. I wondered if my mother would come. Or even my father. My mother came every day; my father came when he could get away from the office. I drowsed in the warm bath of afternoon sun. Nothing mattered.

Then two men came. They talked around me, loading me onto a bed and pushed me down the corridor, through the girls' ward. I saw Trish there. She was my age, with dark black hair and a red curved mouth. I knew her from church. My father told me he had known her mother at university. The mother also had dark hair and was tall. Two days before, I had seen Trish being bathed. She sat up in bed; they took off her top revealing round breasts appended to her chest, with nipples that snagged my eye.

'Good luck,' she said as my bed went past. I wondered if she knew I'd seen her titties. I knew something about her she didn't know I knew. It made me trembly. I didn't know if I would see her again. Maybe I'd never wake up. I tried to smile, bravely.

'You must be brave,' my mother always said. 'Everyone's got something wrong with them. I had to wear boots when I was small because my ankles were weak.' She looked at me. She thought this would make me feel better. People did. When I was in plaster, they would tell me about their colds and headaches. I didn't have ankles. Dr Jock, who seldom smiled but had a kind voice, had taken them out when I was a baby.

'He used to complain that you were too fat,' my mother said. 'We lived far out of town and you used to kick off your plasters, so we would have to drive into town. In the Citroen. "He's too fat," Jock said.'

I didn't remember the farm but I had seen photographs. Of Hamlet, the Great Dane. 'You said your first words to him,' Mother said. 'You said: "Gow, Gagga."' She smiled. I felt embarrassed. She showed me a photograph of myself sitting with my hair brushed up – 'like a mango-pip' – on my father's lap. He was young, sat erect, hands resting around me, not on me, and wore khaki from the war. He had a neatly shaped moustache. When he kissed me it was uncomfortable; and it made him look fierce and angry. In the photograph I scowled. That pear-shaped baby had nothing to do with me. My feet were covered. My little sister Vinnie wasn't born then, only Norline who was five years older and sent to boarding school.

Every six months, we would go to town to see Dr Jock. Usually my father would take the day off from the office and he and I would drive silently into town where everyone was busy and the buildings tall and there were no trees. We would travel up in the lift where the squinty man pressed shiny brass buttons and held the cage door open for you. He was

Afrikaans. Miss Aiken, Dr Jock's secretary, sat in a small room at a desk with a typewriter, telephone and an expectant face. She had a button face and black spectacles and when she tried to kiss me she smelt of clothes that had been hanging too long in the cupboard. Dr Jock would phone her from his desk and when she spoke, she said, 'Yes, doctor, yes, doctor,' a lot. My father did not call him 'Dr Jock' as I did but 'Mr Edelstein'.

'Why do you call him "Mr"?' I asked.

'Because he's a specialist,' he replied. 'You call specialists "Mr" not "Dr".'

'Must I call him "Mr Jock" then?'

Maybe I'd been calling him the wrong name and he was angry with me which is why he never smiled.

Dr Jock's office was dim, with heavy books and wood and a smell of cigars. The walls had placards with Latin and big silver seals.

'Take off your trousers and walk up and down. There.' He gestured with his cigar. My father sat beside his desk.

If you have something wrong with your feet, you have to keep on taking off your trousers. I walked up and down carefully, measuring each step, trying hard.

'Walk as you normally would.'

I couldn't remember how that was but tried and he grunted. He and my father would watch.

'Again.'

Then to my father: 'You see?'

'Mmm.'

Then I had to stand on a glass table, with a mirror beneath, experiencing the chill of the glass, and the warmth of his hand holding me steady as I got up.

'All right,' he would say and this was the signal for me to put on my trousers and leave my father behind in his room. Miss Aiken would give me a sweet and try to talk to me ('Do you like school?'), then my father would come out, looking severe. He often looked severe. I was scared of him and thought he didn't like me because I didn't play games like other boys. He didn't play games like other boys' fathers, who were hearty and hairy. My father was slim, bespectacled and brainy. At school we mocked the small brainy boys with glasses. They were sissies. I didn't like to think my dad was a sissy.

Outside in the sunlight, he talked for the first time. 'You're going to have to have two ops. One on each foot. Sorry, Butch.'

'What about school?'

'You'll have to miss a term. But you'll catch up.'

I wasn't worried about lessons.

That time, when I saw Trish's breasts, it was in the middle of my second last year at prep school. I was going to be a prefect and I didn't want to be away from school. I hadn't been in hospital for two years. It was unfair. Other times I was relieved to go to hospital. I didn't have to go to Latin with Colly, who beat you with the back of a wooden hairbrush. Or have Maths with Mr Long ('Shorty') who had an artificial leg from the war and his hair slicked back. He never spoke to me: I think he disliked me because I also had something wrong with my feet. He wanted to be the only one.

My father continued: 'Jock's got a chap from London coming out. He wants a second opinion. We're going to his house on Saturday.' So I couldn't go and play with Barry across the road.

Jock was wearing light casual trousers. His stomach bulged over the belt. Miss Aiken wasn't there. The house stood among big old green trees and it had slopes you could run up and down on, if you could run. I wouldn't be able to run. The trees at our house were just beginning to grow; the sand yellow and glinty with quartz and mica. A swimming pool that my father had built during his leave, with two Africans, their heads daily getting lower and lower in the ground. The pool echoed the sunlight.

My father had long leave, so he was there every day. I wished he'd be back at work. I didn't like having him there the whole time. Then he built change rooms of creosoted wood beside the pool, and a fence. One for girls, one for boys. The slats weren't very close and I was ashamed of him because he could not make them tight. When the girls went in they'd always say: 'Don't peek,' but we did and they screamed and put towels round themselves. They never tried to see us undressing.

Jock said: 'This is Donna. Why don't you go and play while we talk.' Donna was my age and very pretty.

'Come,' she said. We ran into the trees. They were cool and dark. The jacarandas were shedding blue flowers which popped as we walked.

'Do they have honey in them?' I asked.

'Dunno. Let's try.'

So we sat down on a hillock, out of sight of the house. The sky was getting grey and dark; the air smelt of rain and the jacarandas were bright. We put our tongues into their mauve passages but could not taste honey. We talked and talked and then I heard Jock calling.

'You've got to go,' Donna said solemnly.

'Maybe I've got to have an operation in London,' I said distractedly. 'I don't want to. Not now, I mean.'

Jock called again, more impatiently. Donna twisted her mouth.

'Maybe I can come in with you,' Donna said. 'Just to be there,' she added in case I thought she was babying me.

But he wouldn't let her. And when I had taken off my trousers, walked up and down, and when the English surgeon had finished 'manipulating' my feet silently and I had been asked to leave the room and go and play while they discussed things, it was raining heavily and thundering. Clearly, she wasn't outside in the summer thunderstorm and I didn't know where she was. And then it was time to go home.

But I didn't go to Great Ormond Street Hospital in London, I went back to the Johannesburg Children's Hospital again. And with the two men once again pushing me on the trolley and people staring down at me in the light, I was deposited at the entrance of the operating theatre, green paint and polished floors. The two doors opened and a figure in green robes and a mask looked at me.

'Hello Rob,' he said. It was Jock. I wanted to ask him about Donna but there wasn't time. The big bright globe looked down on the narrow table. I was lifted off. Nurses and the anaesthetist were there. Many eyes watching above masks.

The anaesthetist said: 'Now you're going to have a little sleep. Clench your fist and count to ten.'

He injected me and I started counting quietly: 'One, two, three . . .'

'Count,' he said. I felt irritated and said: 'I *am*.' And then I was out, a damp wet cloth of nothingness rising up my throat.

You can't remember pain, only the experience of having been in pain. I remember a sore throat and thrashing with thirst, and my mother's voice: 'Be calm, I'm here, hush, hush, hush.'

'I'm sore.'

'Hush, hush.'

'I'm thirsty.'

'Can he have some water, nurse?'

'A teaspoonful.'

She gave me a teaspoonful. I was sick, vomiting.

'It's the anaesthetic.'

Later my father came. I was moaning. I had a big hump, like John, over where my feet had been. Maybe they had cut them off to throw them in the fire that made the ward so warm.

'Remember Douglas Bader,' my father said at one stage. He always wanted me to remember Douglas Bader and be brave. But I was sore, a slicing green pain in my feet, and a red rough grainy pain in my throat. I moved my head back and forth, back and forth, trying to shake pain out maybe, maybe trying to settle outrage into rhythm. The night was very long; I eventually slept and when I woke my parents weren't there. Huddy, the koala, was next to my bed. The little boy in the adjoining bed had wanted to sleep with him one night but I didn't want him to. He would come back smelling strange. My mother looked sad when I refused.

'Huddy didn't want to go,' I told her. 'I'd asked him.' She didn't respond. Often she asked me about the bears, what they were doing or thinking. This time she didn't play.

The next day I was sore again. The visitors' bell went and people came in. I looked for my mother but she wasn't there. The rush of people separated, going to different beds. A few latecomers filtered in. My mother still wasn't there. I closed my eyes and tried to sleep away the pain. Maybe the nurse would give me another injection. Why wasn't my mother there? The nurses were all out of the ward. I thought of calling but all the people there would stare. I hated people staring.

'Stare, stare, like a bear,' my sister and I would say aggressively.

'Doesn't he talk nice?' a woman in the street said to my mother once. 'So English.'

Then my mother came. I would not speak to her. 'I'm so sorry I'm late but I had to fetch the girls at school. Daddy can't come today; he's got a meeting.' I didn't say anything.

'How are you feeling?' She leaned forward and kissed me. I turned my head away. She sat down. 'Do you need anything?' I said nothing. How could she be late?

So for an hour, she sat in silence beside the bed. When the bell went, she stood up, a torn look on her face. 'I am sorry; I couldn't help it. Say goodbye.' I said nothing. 'I'll be back tomorrow,' she said. 'Won't you talk to me?' I said nothing. I wanted to but I couldn't. She left, her brisk footsteps tapping the polished floor of the ward, down past Trish in the girls' ward, past the babies that cried when birds flew in and were trapped; out.

I wanted to cry but I couldn't.

I came home after six days. The nurse who had bet me was waiting at the entrance with a Coke.

'See you,' she said.

'Maybe not,' I said smartly.

After the operation, I had to be in bed a long time: six weeks. Most of the time I read or listened to the radio or made plastic models of fighter aircraft: Hurricanes that helped win the Battle of Britain and were slower than Spitfires, Messerschmidt 109s which were very fast, Fokke Wulfes, Mustangs, Sunderlands, Dorniers that were bombers, Junkers 88s that had a lot of glass on their noses, Lancasters, Catalinas with their wings above their hulls, Stukas which were divebombers with screaming sirens to frighten the people they would bomb. My father hung them from the roof; they turned in the wind, a flock in unending, mimicked battle. My mother was out all day and when she came back I asked her if she had brought me models to make.

My little sister Vinnie, and my big sister Norline, went to and from school, returning with the smell of activity, a mingling of sweat and bread. Norline had boyfriends and didn't stay long; Vinnie and I played bears.

One night there was a broadcast of *Great Expectations*. When Pip met Miss Havisham, I thought of Donna. When Magwich loomed out at Pip, I was scared but everyone was downstairs.

My father came home from work and sat at the end of my bed and said: 'How're you, boy?'

'Fine,' I said, and there wasn't much else so he went downstairs to rattle the newspapers and complain about the bloody engineers he worked with. A servant brought me trays with food. A servant picked me up in the evening and took me to the bathroom. I felt awkward, naked in his arms as he deposited me into the bath, sitting sideways so my plasters would be out of the water, feeling the edges soften with time. Some nights before supper, a servant would take me downstairs to sit in the lounge with the rest of the family, my feet up on a stool. But mostly I heard them having supper in the formal red and carved-wood dining room downstairs. Outside the bow windows were two lemon trees. In spring they blossomed, and I could smell the blossom, and hear the family talking.

Once a friend from school visited, Caveman. His mother made him come, he said. I asked him about school and he said that Chicken had got flogged by Collie, the headmaster, for cheating. Our school had won cricket against another school. The new boys were stroppy. I didn't know what he meant. 'Cheeky,' he said impatiently. They had begun to talk differently since I was away, I thought. He'd met this really great chick and was going to a party with her. 'Oh, I forgot, my mom bought this and said I must give it to you.' It was a plastic model kit of a Junkers. I had one already. 'Thanks, hey,' I said. Then we didn't have much more to say.

Friends of my parents came to visit. They always brought presents. They sat for a while in my bedroom, then went downstairs for drinks. I wondered about Trish and Donna. My cousins came to visit: Bridget who was athletic, Wendy who never smiled, and Prissy who was retarded and thought I was her best friend. And Hermene, their mother, whom my father called Calamity Jane because she was always getting married and then fleeing her husband.

Soon after she came back from Texas, with a big hat and leather trousers, she married Danny Levine. Danny always had a deal going on; he was thick-set and talked loudly. My mother said he was a 'Yid' and then told me I was never, but never, to call anyone that.

Hermene then left Danny. She moved in with us – the three girls were at boarding school – and Danny came looking for her. He drove a red Jaguar.

'That proves he's a spiv. Red!' my mother said. He drove urgently into our driveway and my mother said: 'Lock the door.' He got out looking furious and beat at the door.

'Let's throw water at him,' my mother said, so we did. He drove away, still yelling.

Bridget had a hard profile and spoke with an accent from Pietersburg, where she'd grown up.

'Do you know about French-kissing?' she asked me.

'Uh-uh,' I shook my head.

She put her face close to mine and I felt this slobbery thing in my mouth, moving about behind my teeth. I couldn't breathe and I couldn't get away from her either. Her face was looking triumphant.

'That's French-kissing,' she said. 'It's very sexy.'

'Uh, uh,' I contradicted her, getting my breath.

Before the operation, I had played cricket and football. Everyone did. Okay, when I scored a run, someone had to run for me and had to be persuaded that I would decide when to run. And when I played football, it was mostly as goalie and occasionally as full-back. But at least I qualified – as one of the boys, one of the team, a member of the school, a promising South African.

Dr Jock warned me when he took my second set of plasters off, I wouldn't be able to run. He took big shiny scissors and inserted one blade down the plaster and crunched the two blades together. Then he came to the foot and moved more slowly. The blades whispered, mouthing my scar. I wondered if he would cut me. Then he inserted a clamp either side of the cut and cracked the plaster apart. My foot, white and shrunken, lay in bloodstained cotton wool, the skin peeling in the shape of water on the beach. A red cut ran on the inside of the foot, another on the back. It was the echo of a knife.

I don't know what he had done but he was pleased with the new-shape feet, with their raw scars and dots where the stitches had been and the flaking skin. When I tried standing, they felt like jelly. Every night, my mother rubbed in olive oil. Vinnie sat beside the bed and wrapped one of the koala's feet in socks. I could see the koala didn't like it because it hindered his tree-climbing but it made Vinnie happy.

I wouldn't be able to run. I'd have to learn to walk again, one step at a time; thoughts about moving the foot that my foot could not act upon; resistance in my toes, a fear that they might suddenly collapse. Always, the anxiety about falling while I learned a new map of sites of pain, stiffness or simple incapacity.

Because I couldn't play cricket, the headmaster, probably acting on suggestions from my father, encouraged me to swim. I swam breaststroke in the swimming gala, walking out of the change room in my bathing costume, aware – or imagining that everyone was aware – of thin, withered legs. I bulged above them, hearing silence among the spectators, then the whispering. People applauded tentatively as I stood, waiting for the starter's gun. With enormous flair, I dived in and stayed underwater for as long as I could, coming up to the sound of cheering and the sight of the other contestants half a length ahead of me. Three minutes after they ended the race, I was still flapping my arms through the water, legs trailing like someone else's load. They started applauding as I got out. I wanted to run – well, walk very fast – to the change rooms. Maybe find a machine gun there to mow them all down.

'Well done, my boy,' said Collie, our headmaster, coming into the change room where I sat with face marked as much by exertion as humiliation.

Collie was very English. He had a hard, beady eye: when you were fooling around in class, you suddenly became aware of his glare from the stairs overlooking the window. He would march in, speak briefly to the master in charge, then crook his finger at you. You'd have to walk round the school with him in front, to the study where, still silent, he would gesture to you to bend down, and flog you with the back of a clothes brush.

51

'Now go back to class,' he would say, in case you were thinking of leaving the school. Whenever people beat you, they had to say something afterwards. A joke to make you like them. A lecture when all you wanted to do was leave and rub your bum. Something. It helped them, I suppose.

'I came last.' 'Sir,' I added. The small boys at school thought his name was 'Sir'. Mr Sir, they called him to each other.

'You did your best. You're excused from games. But you must watch them. School spirit.'

Every break, the others played on the fields, running and shouting. I started reading every break, finding a bench under the pin-oaks, whose shells made piercing whistles. I read *A Summer Place*, about a cold island in Maine, and a boy who was left out of the gang, a pretty girl, an acrid handyman and his baying dog on snow-stormy nights. And a picture on the cover of Johnny and Molly, hand in hand, walking towards the sea at night. I stared and stared at the picture, and thought about Angela who lived across the road and was pretty, though once when she put her face close to mine, her breath smelt sulphuric. Afterwards whenever she came near, I would not breathe.

I went back to class, walking painfully, a step at a time, considering each movement. The hair on my balls was growing again, coarsely. I could not discuss games with the others and learned Latin, 'Amo, amas, amat . . .' assiduously. Had nightmares of hospital. The koalas were ranged in a row in my room. We did not talk much anymore. Next year I would be going to boarding school, far away. It would be better. Maybe I would play cricket and run or come first in swimming. Maybe I would meet Donna or Trish or Angie in the holidays. Maybe I'd have no more operations. Maybe it would all be better.

# Identity Scribbled in Strife

*Zanele Dolly Simelane*

Being mocked by mockery itself
Dwelling in my state
Forgiven by the weather that harms and protects
Bemused by my lingering lapses of time
A sense of overcoming massages my desires.

# On Amputation
## *Jillian Hamilton*

see the soot
once my foot

soot foot
foot soot

once earthbound
now flying

flying sooty foot
foot of flying soot

where will you go on your flight
where will you go
after rising smudgily
from the chimney
that sends you on your epic journey
an airborne journey
far beyond the imaginings
of an earth fixed foot

fly away sooty foot

(mary had a little lamb
his feet were black as soot
and everywhere that mary went
his sooty foot he poot)

# 'shore with no feet'
## Kobus Moolman

(from *Separating the Seas*)

shore with no feet.

the light off the wind
green and cold with wings
and a voice that sounds
like echoing in glass.

bridge with no handhold

and two faithless feet;
a cracked stick to prop
the night up with eyes;
indiscernible tides of salt

and rocks without ever anyone.

# A New Dream Emerges
*Musa Zulu*

(from *The Language Of Me*)

PARALYSIS... I WAS paralysed! It was a devastating realisation. It is hard to describe the feelings that went through me, the depth of my despair, how lost and alone I felt. I did not want to believe that such a thing had happened to me. Young as I was, I had already accomplished so much in my life and was looking forward to achieving so much more. I was at the peak of my potential, in the process of spreading my wings for still greater heights. My goal was to vault into the skies and shine up there with all the other stars. It was a crushing blow to realise that those big ambitions had died in the wreck along with the person I used to be. 'What about my dreams – is this where the road ends for me?' was all I could think of. I only had questions, but no solutions, nor any sense of direction to guide me out of my present crisis. I suppose I was just reeling from the blow, drowning in the pool of my own fears. It's not every day that you are faced with change on such a scale and it's hard to maintain equilibrium and an optimistic outlook under such circumstances. I used to cry a lot during those early days – most of the time alone, so as to hide my pain from others. It was all so strange and confusing.

I could not feel my lower body at all. My legs were numb and cold as ice. I had no control over my bladder and bowels. I was on a permanent catheter and had to wear a nappy – I was torn apart by the indignity of my condition and the helplessness I felt. There was a button next to my bed that I had to press to summon a staff member when I had messed myself, and every time it happened, I just could not bring myself to make the move. Finally, I would find the courage and with quaking hands press for help. Every time the nurses came to change my nappy and bedding, I would lie there frozen and wish for the moment to pass quickly. The nurses were always kind, but I couldn't deal with the fact that my privacy was suddenly invaded and my pride shattered. I would lie in my shame and wonder if that's the way a child feels every time he or she messes up – except that I was 23 years old! Every minute of every day I was confronted by some new and traumatic revelation. I was devastated to learn that I had also lost my erection in the accident. Short of a miracle, it was another loss I was going to have to live with for the rest of my life, and the pain of that realisation was not easy to take.

Early morning bed-baths, physiotherapists, occupational therapists, psychologists, neurologists, medical specialists and their assistants; white walls and ever-clean lab coats, tilt-tables and parallel bars, catheters and suppositories, X-rays and thermometers, multiple scans and timed visits . . . persistent wails and death in the ward. These were the elements that made up my days – not my version of an ideal world! Nobody wants to live in a place where death and life are continually balanced on the scales, and that has been my experience of what defines a hospital. In that place, there was constant pain and uncertainty, and the only thing that ever seemed to make any of the patients smile from the heart was the moment when they were discharged. I am scared of hospitals. I hate the way that control is taken away from you there. In that world, not much seems to be perceived as a positive sign. You wake up sad one morning and they say you are depressed; you wake up feeling more cheerful the following day and somebody says you are exhibiting signs of schizophrenia – you can almost hear their minds whispering 'denial'. You are constantly labelled and tagged. I hated living as a 'case': 'Sister, how is "he" today?' You become a third person in your very presence. 'Tell him such and such and make sure he takes this medication once in the morning and once before he sleeps.' My life was suddenly placed in someone else's hands in the name of care, my independence taken away from me. I felt I had lost myself. I was half out of my mind with fury at my situation, carried through the days on the waves of my frustration.

I have never been one for confines – the outside world is my home, my space. Now, day after day, I was in bed, inside a ward with virtually no colour, no visual stimulation, where almost everything was white, from the ceiling above my head to the tiles on the floor below the white bed – all much too clean and antiseptic for an outdoors boy like me. All I wanted was to walk out that door back to my familiar 'pig-sty' at home. Even the food was very different from what I was used to in taste and appearance. The mood and the air were always cold. I take my hat off to the healthcare workers of the world for the hard work they put into trying to make those places a normal environment, where people can embrace the hope that they will live to see the next day in. Not that I was even in a bad hospital. Since I was fortunate enough to be on medical aid when the accident happened, the ambulance crew took me straight to a private health facility. This was Entabeni, a private hospital of world-class standard, where everything possible is done to ensure the highest levels of health and recovery. All the facilities were there to give a solid foundation to the long-term rehabilitation programme that would be implemented in the days ahead.

I remember my reaction when the wheelchair first came – I cried my soul out. 'God, why have you forsaken me?' Questions and endless tears! The nursing staff helped me up and placed me on this 'object'. I hated it with all my heart – to me it represented my helplessness. My pride made it difficult for me to accept. I could not deal with the prospect of being seen riding on that thing by people who had known me during my able-bodied days. I kept being told everything would be 'fine' – but to me, that wheelchair tolled the bells of my final moment. I was so traumatised by the thought of lifelong paralysis that I believed I was literally going to die. At night, I had recurring bad dreams where I was drowning in the bathtub. My legs were paralysed and my arms too weak to pull me up and save me from the danger – I would actually see myself slipping away underwater. It was a terrible nightmare. When I woke up there would be beads of sweat running down my forehead. I know now that the dream represented the helplessness I was feeling, but at the time, it all seemed terribly real. I would lie there dead scared – convinced it could really happen and that it would be the end of me. I longed to go home where I knew I would be safe with the people that loved me. I was very lonely in that hospital ward, a stranger in a strange world – isolated from my own identity and the vital energy of society. I admit I wasn't an ideal patient. I threw a few tantrums and boycotted meals in protest. It was the only way I could express my frustration at the situation in which I found myself. In a short space of time, my temper had created bad blood between me and some of the nursing staff.

One of the most devastating things about paralysis is the way it impacts on normal bodily functions. Because I could no longer urinate in the normal way, I had to use a catheter to empty my bladder. The first few days, I was hooked up to a permanent tube. Then I graduated to the disposable kind, which I was supposed to insert myself. I hated that bloody catheter. It became my worst enemy. I found it completely humiliating to have to fiddle with myself, poking about in my penis, trying to insert the tube into the right channel. It was like puncturing the very essence of your manhood, tampering with the core of you. I made up my mind to boycott it, convinced there had to be another way. With my very limited understanding of human anatomy, it seemed to me that if water could pass into my bladder unaided, it must eventually, by the sheer pressure of its own gravity, expel itself unaided. I decided to conduct a little experiment to prove my theory. After two days of not urinating, my bladder swelled up till I looked like someone in the early stages of pregnancy. My doctor wasn't happy with what I was doing, warning me that I was creating a serious risk of infection, with all the complications this would bring. But I stubbornly persevered. On the third day, I woke up to find the bed soaking wet and my bladder blissfully empty. I lay there laughing in joy. My small triumph over the catheter signalled a much bigger victory in other ways. The lesson it taught me was to work with and listen to my body. After three months of battling through this messy procedure of allowing my bladder to fill naturally and then pressurise itself to empty naturally, I began to get control over the process. I started to feel the subtle pulsating that warned me my bladder needed to empty itself. Through this experience, my mind learnt to attune itself to other signals too, the slight spasms in the legs, the tingling sensations in the feet that indicated that all was not as it should be. In this way, I developed a much more harmonious relationship with my body in general, and my capacity for sensation has come back to an amazing degree.

One of the things I found so difficult about being bedridden was that aside from the paralysis and a few minor injuries sustained in the accident, I was in good health. My body was incapacitated, but free from pain and full of vitality, and my mind was still operating with all its former drive and energy. One of the big frustrations eating at me was the belief that I was doomed to a wheelchair's pace of locomotion forever. When I first learnt I was paralysed, I was terrified by the thought that my driving days were over. My family showed me photographs of my beloved Golf, which I had been driving at the time of the crash. I was horrified by the wreckage I saw and completely devastated by the thought that it had been my first and last car. I had loved that Golf like a part of me. I bought it on

30 August 1994 and the very next day it emerged from a Car Audio Shop, equipped with an uncompromising sound system. Off we went together – a marriage made in boys' heaven. I cared for that car with absolute dedication, kept it polished, vacuumed and serviced – in mint condition. The two of us had a wonderful relationship that was tragically terminated after only nine months by the collision with the fateful brick wall. We both suffered the heavy blows of impact and my baby was towed away to a scrapyard while I was being wheeled into the ICU – two lives forever separated.

As the days of bedridden immobility rolled by, all I wanted to do was get up, walk back into my life, find myself another car and drive away to my dreams. I was terribly frustrated by the thought that my crucial independence had been permanently revoked. This was why I hated the wheelchair so much – it could never substitute for the class of wheels I loved. When a gorgeous occupational therapist visited me at Entabeni Hospital one day the first question I posed to her was: 'Will I ever be able to drive a car again?' When she said 'yes' with a bright smile and explained how it was possible, relief gushed through me. I had never seen anyone in a wheelchair driving a car and up to that point had no idea that it was even a viable option. I came to see for myself just how possible it was when, a short while later, I met Vusi Ndimeni, a compassionate stranger who took an interest in me and was later to become my good friend and brother. Our meeting was one of those fortunate coincidences that life throws across your path. It was a few months after the crash, and I was experiencing severe pains down my back. Since I had already left the hospital, a friend recommended I see a chiropractor, so I made an appointment and got someone to take me along. Wheeling myself into the consultation room, I noticed an African guy sitting on a sofa. We did not even greet each other, and when I came out he was gone. A lady at the reception desk informed me that 'the stranger' had asked for my number so he could phone me later. I asked why he wanted to contact me, but all she said was, 'He just wants to talk to you.' Later that evening 'a Vusi' called and told me that he was also in a wheelchair. He remarked that he could not help but notice the sorrow that was registered all over my face. Strangely enough, it did not even occur to me to tell him to go to hell, which was my favourite response at that time to anyone in a wheelchair who tried to come close to me. Instead, I opened up and told Vusi that I was not fine. I confided to this stranger that my life was a mess and that the changes I was faced with had completely demolished me. All of this I said with tears streaming down my face. Vusi's response was: 'All will be fine with time.' It was the same response I'd heard over and over again from others and it usually sent me into a rage. But in Vusi's mouth, it sounded different. He had really listened to my pain. He knew what it was to be in the place I was in, and when he told me everything would be all right, I believed him.

Vusi's paralysis was the result of a bullet hitting his spine in an incident related to his work with prisoners. He was strong, positive and reassuring. He told me that it only needed positive thinking for me to make it through this disaster. The sincerity in his voice was very convincing and there was something about him that I could not ignore. I felt very comfortable talking with him and found security in knowing that there was someone out there who had felt and understood my pain. He invited me to his home to meet his wife and child. The following day, my brothers took me to his house in the grounds of Westville Prison, where he worked as a prison warder. It was during that visit that things fell into place for me. Vusi was driving a maroon BMW 325i, complete with sports kit and a low suspension that exaggerated its sleek, sporty lines – a real beauty specially designed to meet his needs. He took me for a drive and later allowed me to try the mounted hand controls. When I drove that car, it was like heaven had opened its doors for me to come in and rest in peace.

I knew then that it was completely possible for me to drive, despite my paralysis, and the new dream I started to embrace right then and there was to get my own wheels and drive myself wherever I wanted to go.

After a full month of being confined to my hospital bed, I had my first chance to venture into the outside world. I was given a weekend pass-out, which allowed me to spend the weekend at home and return to the hospital on Monday morning. The date was 20 May – I remember it well because it was the same day that I heard on the news that actor Christopher Reeves, the Superman hero, had broken his neck in a horse-riding accident. My friend Bonga Mlambo collected me, driving a car identical to the Golf in which I had crashed. It was a freaky coincidence and it unsettled me terribly. I clearly remember the fear I felt of being in that car, made worse by my lack of physical control. I had minimal balance at that time, very little command over my posture. As we drove away from the hospital, the first place I asked to be taken to was the infamous 'wall' – the crash site in Umbilo Road. It was a strange feeling of *déjà vu* to be recreating the fateful journey in the identical car. I still had absolutely no memory of what had happened, yet in the space of a month, my whole life had turned upside down.

Arriving home was a very moving experience. My brothers (I include my close cousins in the term) were overjoyed to see me. We sat and chatted on the balcony like old times. But when darkness fell, they had to take me inside. My body thermostat had gone completely haywire. Even though the evening was warm, I was freezing, unable to warm up no matter how many blankets they piled on me. That visit home started me thinking deeply. So much had changed in the time of my absence; I no longer had the freedom of the house. I watched my brothers bounding up and down the stairs that lead to the outside room we had shared and felt for the first time the cruel contrast between their freedom of movement and my confinement. I was no longer master of my own fate. If I wanted something, someone had to fetch it for me. If I wanted to go to bed, somebody had to carry me there. It was during that weekend that it truly dawned on me that this was not a temporary state of affairs, but my permanent condition. I remember that I started to cry. The next day, the whole family came to see me; they gathered around me – my father, mother, sisters, and brothers – solicitous and loving, so eager to be of service, to fetch me this or do that for me. I was completely touched by their loving attention. I wasn't used to being the family focal point. They were behaving like the admiring audiences who used to gather round me during my Michael Jackson days to watch my dancing displays. In some ways, their loving attention made my new situation even harder to bear. But it was a good pain – a reminder to me that I wasn't alone, but part of a loving community.

'Tilling the Hard Soil' – William Zulu

# Bat Magic
## *Heinrich Wagner*

*On stage there is a table, flanked by two chairs, with one chair behind it. Music plays.*
*Lights down to total blackout. Voice with echo.*

Good evening and welcome to another pre-birth ceremony. The ritual for this evening won't be new to you, you've lived with our results through and through. To remind you of the date, it is 23 May 1972. I have a few accolades to hand out to a number of children to be born tomorrow morning.

At 5 a.m. sharp, Paul Adam Thompson. Paul, you will never have to listen for you will be as deaf as a doornail for the rest of your life.

One minute later, Robert John Tires. Robert, you will never have to look for a chair for you will be in a wheelchair for the rest of your life.

One minute later. George van der Boss. George, you will never be challenged mentally for you will be mentally challenged for the rest of your life.

One minute later, Heinrich Wagner. Hein, you will never see anything beautiful or ugly for you will be as blind as a bat for the rest of your life.

Thank you and have a good life.

[*Lights up. Hein walks in, stumbles over chair. Recovers, steadies himself, one foot on the chair*]

The only thing I've seen before is stars – and that happened the last time I unexpectedly knocked my head against something.

When the Swedish band Roxette released the song 'Crash Boom Bang', I thought it was a special dedication to all blind people without guide dogs who kept walking into things. Apparently not; it is a special dedication to Steve Hofmeyer, because every time he falls in love: crash boom pram.

It is strange how people always ask me, 'So, how did it happen? Was IT an accident? Have you always been like THIS?' Like what exactly? Let's say I went blind yesterday, would they feel more sorry for me? Or is it a way of measuring how patronising they should be throughout the rest of the conversation?

From a very young age I knew that I could not see and I also knew that if I wasn't focused on where I was going and what I was doing I would get lost or fall over or fall off things. This was painfully demonstrated to me on a number of occasions before I truly believed it.

Actually society labels people like me blind. However – [*Takes centre stage*] I can see clearly now! At the age of four and a half my parents decided to send me to the Worcester school for the blind, Pioneer School. The only school at the time that could possibly cope with blind kids. Reflecting on that time I can still feel the fabric of my mother's trousers between my fingers as I was trying desperately to hang on to them, when she was about to leave me behind in that unknown place of total darkness. Remember that at home I could easily find my way to the kitchen, [*Moves around chair, to the table, back to the other chair*] walk to the bathroom and find my way back to my most comfortable and secure place: my bedroom. The deep, dark cave I never wanted to leave to face the light.

So there I was in a boarding house with hundreds of other blind kids, and some that really believed they could actually see! Yes, some still had sight but they certainly believed it was more than they actually had. Others were totally blind and under the illusion they could see pretty well and, well, a number of kids like myself, who were 'totals' and knew it. I soon discovered the other totals were making all sorts of funny noises when walking down the passage [*Bangs on table*] or outside in the school grounds [*Clicks*]. The clicking of the tongue or fingers and the slapping of the hand on the leg. This generated sufficient noise to worn other blindies that there is a total in transit! The other benefit I only discovered a little later is that by listening to the reflection of the sounds off walls and trees, you can successfully navigate [*Navigates around table*] yourself around obstacles.

Once I developed the skill myself I could not wait to get home and get onto my brother's bicycle, [*Mimes bicycle*] and try to cycle up and down our driveway without injury by using the new navigation skill I call bat magic. I just desperately wanted to be like all the other kids. I dreamed about doing normal things every day. Riding my brother's bicycle, at high speeds, on my own was one of the first goals I can remember setting for myself. After a few weekends' practice I was able to cycle around the crescent we lived in without hitting the pavement once. [*Mimes cycling*] By listening to the reflection of the bicycle's noise off the pavement I could cycle in a straight line without major difficulty. I certainly had to be totally focused at all times or make my way to the bathroom to stock up on some plasters. I soon discovered that my life would be one of navigating through the confused world of the sighted. Every school holiday when I arrived home and took out my brother's bicycle I could hear our neighbours warning one another not to park in the road 'because that mad blind kid is at home again'.

[*Sound byte*]

Three hundred blind kids in one school; that, believe me, could lead to trouble. Especially if half of them think they can see. I remember teaching myself survival techniques at a very early age. Every evening at the dinner table when the headmaster said 'close your eyes let's pray', I thought to myself, why do you continually want to remind us we cannot see? When he started praying I used to grab my fork and begin to stab in the air all around my plate [*Stabs table around plate*] because guaranteed some one-eyed twilight monster would try to steal something off my plate. What a great experience it was; nowhere else in the world can you give someone an up-yours without any severe reaction. Beside the 300 totals and half-blind kids, the school was pretty much similar to an ordinary school for sighted kids. They taught us Braille instead of the normal writing skills. The syllabus from Grade One to Matric was exactly the same as a mainstream school. But, although the syllabus was the same, that does not suggest that sighted people know about or treat blind people as if they are ordinary citizens and are just aiming to make a valuable contribution to society.

Since I can remember, I hated being patronised by anyone. I think it goes back to the day the mother of a friend of mine kept asking 'him' if 'he' would like some tea. Must I cut his bread? Shame, does 'he' want some sugar or milk in his tea? At the time I thought to myself why are you not concerned about the real things in life, such as 'Johnny, do you think he likes your sister? Johnny, do you think he knows how to kiss?' That day I realised there is a hell of a lot to be done to market the abilities of blind people! We are normal, the fact that our eyes don't work that well does not suggest that we are mentally challenged or deaf!

My parents were very active in the sporting community, and my brother and I spent most holidays visiting our grandparents. My granny used to feed me an extraordinary amount of carrots. Sliced carrots, grated carrots, chopped carrots, carrot cake, raw carrots, over-cooked carrots, sugar-dipped carrots, carrot-coated sweets, carrots out of my ears! Only later in life did I discover that she had been trying to improve my eyesight! God bless her soul. [*Prayerful gesture*]

At the age of fourteen or fifteen I had many fights with God in my mind, for I had to find someone to blame for my situation. At the same time I often had stand-up fights with God, screaming, swearing and shouting, 'Why me? Why blind? Who do you think you are to make me blind? You, a God of love?' Yes, I was as frustrated as hell.

I can remember sitting at the back of a physiology class halfway through Grade Ten while the teacher was describing the functionality of the eye. Needless to say, I was in dreamland within seconds. A normal teenage boy, dreaming about motorbikes, fast cars, sexy blondes and Castle beer. Suddenly, a question came up in my mind. How many totally blind people are there in the world today? I immediately slipped out of the class and made off to the school library. Thankfully, the teacher was also a total. After some research I discovered that out of twenty-thousand sighted people roughly one person is totally blind! This was one of the biggest discoveries in my life to date. Only one out of twenty-thousand? Yes, yes, yes! I'm special, I'm unique! I'm one out of twenty-thousand sighted people that are totally blind! I made a very big decision that day. I chose to see it as an advantage, a blessing and the most positive fact I've ever discovered in my life.

One of my classmates introduced me to the CB radio [*Mimes using a radio*] and soon I got hooked. 'Any buddy for a copy on the 1-9?' I had CBs in my dad's car, my mother's car, in my bedroom, you name it. What I loved about it was the fact that I could pull faces at the sighted people behind my microphone and they could not see it! I was like a kid with a new toy. My CB handle was POPEYE and believe me I never had big muscles. I soon picked up another youngster on the air and realised he must live very close to my parents' house in Durbanville. After a short chat we decided to have an 'eyeball' down the road from where we lived. Michael did not know that I was totally blind and we stood about five metres away from one another waiting for each other. I couldn't wait any longer and started calling his CB handle. 'C-1, C-1, do you copy, over?' 'Yes, yes, nice to see you.' 'Hi, nice to hear you.'

We became best friends and he was in many ways my anchor in the sighted world. He showed me how to walk cool, how to pull a peace sign, how to change my hairstyle, and a few other things we can discuss later over a few drinks. Michael has always been a very analytical person and tried to understand what it really meant to see nothing. I always asked him to try to describe colours to me. Yes, the grass is green and the sky is blue. However, what do green and blue really look like? Every colour creates an emotion, so they are different for different people. One day he had enough of my colour bullshit and worked a plan. While having breakfast at his house he put a block of ice in my left hand and explained, 'This is blue.' He then, without me knowing, turned on the stove, slapped my other hand on the plate and explained, 'This is red! And don't ever bug me with your colour story again.'

As a youngster I loved motorbikes and most of my sighted friends had one. I was always on the back of one of them dicing someone else, until I convinced Michael that I should sit in front for a change. Being a true friend he understood that I must be desperate to do normal things. And after some initial training with the gears, brakes and the throttle we hit the road. He would sit behind me holding on to my elbows and shout the commands. A little left, a little right, open up, anchors. Oh my God, full brakes! The blind man riding the bike soon became the talk of the town and turned into a party trick after a while.

One day, after a few cooldrinks at my parents' house, we decided to go fetch some videos at Michael's house. Needless to say I was driving again. To this day I do not know what got into Michael's head. For some reason, however, he forgot I couldn't see. We were flying down the back straight to his house and I knew it involved a 70-degree bend to the left. Well, this particular day we kept straight, and went through the fence at roughly 90 kilometres per hour. I spent a few days in hospital undergoing serious plastic surgery because the fence sliced my face rather badly. The scars are up for review after the show. Michael was fine since he was the one wearing the helmet. I never did, because it was impossible to hear the commands from the back when wearing a helmet.

During my Grade Ten year the school decided to embark on a national fundraising project to start up a specialised computer-training centre for blind students. The event they decided upon was to cycle from Johannesburg to Cape Town on tandem bicycles. A half-total in front and a total at the back. Due to my involvement in computers, as well as my love for competitive sports, I was selected as one of the totals to participate.

After six months' training the event kicked off in Johannesburg. My half-blind partner, Danie, was actually a little more than half-blind. What helped the twelve half-blind pilots, however, was a huge luminous orange flag hanging from the back of the kombi that lead the way to Cape Town. We did not take the traditional N1 route to Cape Town, but went through towns such as Kennard, Brandvlei, Klaver, etc. Throughout the event we only had one minor accident and to this day I'm convinced that the kombi was not the only thing leading us. We cycled about 150 kilometres during the day and stayed over in various towns in the evenings on our way to Cape Town.

I specifically remember the night in Klaver. After being on the road for eight days and under twenty-four-hour surveillance by five teachers, another total and myself decided to slip out that evening and hit the town – Klaver. Well, with two long canes ticking away in the night, we eventually discovered the only pub in Klaver. The owner immediately recognised us, for obvious reasons. But we were welcomed in for a drink. He promised not to tell our teachers. Little did we know that one of the teachers was sitting in the pub already, now staring at us. Between the two of us we had about ten rand and after two beers, it was gone. While we were sitting having our drinks, I kept hearing the loud-mouth next to me ordering Olofberg Brandy and I began scheming. As he ordered his third one I asked him if my friend and I might taste his drink. He offered to buy us one, but I insisted on tasting his drink. He agreed and continued talking to his friend while I took a swig of his drink. I had planned the next move with my total friend, and as he received the glass from me he popped his glass eye into the drink. I handed it back to the man and the waiting began. Ting, ting, ting. I could hear the eye at the bottom of the glass and it sounded just like ice. As the man took the last swig the eye at the bottom of the glass rolled over and stared directly at him. He dropped the glass, fell backwards off his chair and fled. The eye ended up behind the bar counter and the poor superstitious barman jumped on top of the fridge. [*Crawls about looking for the eye*] After another fifteen minutes on our hands and knees we managed to retrieve the eye and the rest of the patrons entertained us until early the next morning.

While in boarding school some of the half-blinds and myself occasionally slipped out over weekends to join up with our other total and sighted friends that lived in Worcester. [*Mimes his escape*] This meant we had to climb down the water pipes in order to get down from the second floor. This was rather scary for the pipes were flimsy and to this day I can remember the shape of the trail down from the far left window of the bathroom. The headmaster once told me he saw me climbing up the wall in a dream, but he was very happy when he woke up to find that he was only dreaming! I wonder what he was doing after lights out!
[*Sound byte*]

Since I can remember I have always been interested in the female species. This became more obvious to me throughout my teenage years and I had to consult my sighted friend Michael about the situation. As you can imagine I had many unanswered questions in my mind and an incredibly strong desire to have them verified. I do not suggest that all teenage boys have a good look at *Hustler* and *Playboy* magazines but believe me, if I could at the time, I would've. I still believe publishing a Braille

*Playboy* would be a bestseller in the sighted world, because you could read it with the lights off at night. So Michael did his best to be as descriptive as possible. But the day after he asked his first girlfriend out, he refused to answer any more questions on the subject. So I thought, hmmm, you were also just speculating, and now perhaps you know what it is really about, don't you?

Kissing is a very challenging concept for a total until you've made contact with the girl's mouth. My first few attempts ended on and around the nose. Once you make proper contact though . . .

Why do girls have little bumps around their nipples? It is Braille and it reads, 'Nibble here.'

At the age of sixteen I fell in love with my first girlfriend, Yolanda, a half-blind girl who joined our school when she was about fifteen years old and her eyes had deteriorated to the point where she was forced to start using Braille. We had a steady relationship for about three years until for some reason we decided to go our own ways. It was not cool to have a total partner, especially if you are a total or half-blind yourself. Who will drive the car? Who will do this? Who will do that? Whatever! It is strange to think that I've never seen her but know exactly what she looks like.

During the June school holidays in 1991, about three weeks after we broke off our relationship, I decided to pay her a visit in Johannesburg. The pain of not having her in my life anymore was tremendous! So, with very little money at my disposal and a very strong urge to see her, I decided to hitch-hike from Worcester to Johannesburg. Yes, me, my long cane and I. We hit the N1 to Jo'burg at about three in the morning and within seconds a car pulled off to pick me up. I approached the car with my bag in the one hand and the long cane in the other and as I was about to open the door the person put foot. Well, I could only think that he suspected the long cane was a traditional weapon and this was a hijack in progress. About an hour later another car pulled over and this time I was allowed to jump in. What a strange bunch of people: two Turks, a Russian, a Chinese woman and a Capie. It did not take me long to fall asleep because the cigarettes they smoked had a very lovely smell to them. At Colesberg I woke up and the driver asked me for some money towards petrol. Well, I handed some money to him and it was clearly not enough. A fight broke out between the other passengers and the last thing I heard before I ran stumbling away, was, 'It was your fucking idea to hijack this damn car!'

My next lift took me as far as Winburg and this is where I spent most of the next day alongside the highway. I was now more than halfway to Jo'burg and it was too far to turn around. I must have fallen asleep on my bag next to the road at about midnight, and the next thing I heard was a very loud hooter and tyres squealing in my ears. I dived backwards and at the same time the truck drove over the bag I was sleeping on. What I did not know was that where I'd decided to sleep next to the road was dead centre in a stop-over area for trucks, and fortunately this was the only one that had decided to do so. The driver jumped out and was about to kill me when he realised that I was blind. I think he got a bigger fright than me and he agreed to take me all the way to Jo'burg because it was on his way; only for me to discover on my arrival that Yolanda had already managed to find herself a sighted boyfriend with a car. Well, the same day I jumped a train back to Cape Town and believe me, 22 hours between the toilet and the linen cupboard is painful.

[*Sound byte*]

*RAP, BAT, RAP.*

I'm sure most of you watched some of the Olympic Games that took place in Sydney, Australia, during 2000. Now for those of you that don't know, the Paralympic Games for the funny people starts directly after the event for the not-so funny people.

The administrators of the Paralympic Games are not allowed to discriminate against any entry so, yes, 2000 had a few strange entries. For the 100-metre freestyle swimming event a person without arms, a person without legs, and a head entered the competition. The guy with legs had no problem getting onto the starting block and the guy with the arms managed to climb onto the block with his hands. The head requested that someone roll him into the pool when the gun went off. This was arranged and the race kicked off. The guy with the arms managed to take the lead and at the 50-metre turn he was well ahead of the rest. About five metres before the end he spotted some air bubbles coming up from the bottom of the pool and looking down he saw the head lying on the bottom. He swam down, picked up the head and placed it on the side of the pool. The head started coughing up water and swearing. When the head calmed down the guy with the arms asked him why on earth he had entered such a difficult event, and the head replied: 'I've been practising for the last four years to swim with my ears and five seconds before the gun went off someone pulled a swimming cap over me!'

I trust you realise this isn't part of my autobiography!

Just like any ordinary school the Pioneer School also offered sports such as athletics and swimming, as well as netball and rugby for the kids that could still see a little. The teachers thought the latter was too dangerous for the totals. Well, the totals had to invent their own ball game to satisfy the basic playground needs. We slightly modified a game called '*dryffings*' ('driftings') by placing the ball in a plastic bag. This allowed us to hear where the ball was going. I soon got a team together called the Three Blind Mice and our biggest opposition was the Backstreet Bats. They kept winning and we had to become a little more inventive. One of my team members took a few extra plastic bags onto the field. [*Produces a plastic bag from his pocket*] The next time we played and were behind on the score, he ran up to the middle and shook one of the bags. Once the Backstreet

Bats had run to the middle, we scored with the real ball behind them. [*Scores*] The half-blind rugby team played against the deaf rugby team on a number of occasions. As you can appreciate, the referee had to signal to the deaf when he blew the whistle. The best way of beating them was to pretend that the referee had blown the whistle and then run through and score under the uprights.

I participated in athletics at school and was selected to represent Western Province at the South African Championships three years in a row. I used to participate in field as well as track events. The 100-metres for totals was the most interesting of them all. One person at a time and you have a guide with a megaphone at the finishing line. You start off in lane four and the idea is to stay in lane four. Beyond one and seven is pain. The announcer will keep calling the line number that you are in to keep you in a straight line. My best performance was 12.5 seconds.

Back in August 1992, I remember waking up one morning to a phone call from an old total friend telling me that he had read in a Braille magazine about a sighted guy who wanted to take two 'totals' on the Cape to Rio yacht race. I was a little amused at first, but, being open to any challenge, I made my way to the Royal Cape Yacht Club that Wednesday afternoon. The only sailing I had done at that stage was a cocktail party on a yacht sponsored by the company I was working for at the time.

After three months' training I was selected as one of the blind yachtsmen and worked hard to prepare the yacht for the race. We installed audio equipment on the yacht so that Neels and myself would be able to take the ropes and the helm of the yacht with confidence. During the second week of November that same year our skipper had to charter a yacht to Durban and, very sadly, the yacht went down on the treacherous coast just after Port Elizabeth. He drowned in the incident and may God bless his soul. We were determined to continue with the race in January and the only skipper that we managed to convince to sail with us was a deaf guy. He obviously did not listen to what we were asking him. Well, you can imagine the miscommunication in the beginning. He would frantically point to a rope and Neels and myself would sit and stare into space. He could lip read and whenever you felt like swearing at him you just covered your mouth with your hand. We made it to Rio in 28 days and, well, what an experience. Being 1 400 sea miles from the nearest coastline you realise how small you really are in the world. On this trip I also realised that I can be and do whatever I want if I put my mind to it and am realistic about the end goal. 'If you can conceive it, actively believe it and act upon it, you will achieve it,' said Wayne Dwyer.

In 1996 I got involved in laying the foundations for Blind Cricket South Africa. Yes, you may ask how blind people play cricket? It is the only team sport for blind people out there as far as I know. Blind cricket started in India soon after the Second World War, because a large number of people were blinded during the war. So, how does it work? Blind cricket is very similar to sighted cricket. The only difference is that the people playing it are blind. The team consists of eleven players, four totals and seven half-blinds. We play with a ball that is the same size as a normal cricket ball, made out of plastic with sixteen ball bearings inside. When it moves, it sounds like a giant baby rattle. We also have a few additional gentleman's agreements in place to ensure fair play. When the bowler runs up to deliver the ball, he shouts, 'Play', at the point of delivery. This gives the poor total facing the ball an indication that the ball is on its way. [*Sets up chair as wicket*] In addition, the ball must bounce before it hits the popping crease. This helps the batsman work out the line by listening to where the ball pitches.

The first-ever blind cricket world cup event took place in India in November 1998 and South Africa participated as well as the top six cricket-playing nations, i.e. Australia, India, England, New Zealand, Sri Lanka and Pakistan. At the time we selected the South African team we only had 45 players to select from, while countries such as India and Pakistan had 3 500 and 4 000 players respectively. We had great difficulty fundraising enough money to send the team over. However, my wife and I eventually managed to secure some additional sponsorship. One hundred and sixty blind cricketers from all over the world, well that could only lead to some form of chaos. I recall playing the semi-finals on a cricket field pretty close to a very busy airport in old Deli. Whenever a plane came over we put up a finger and called for bad light! This rule was adopted and added to the rules' list. South Africa went on to win the world cup and this was probably the highlight of my life thus far. I remember walking off the field thinking that I helped to secure the first blind cricket world cup for my country and what an honour it was to be a part of it.

After completing a number of computer training courses during my first year out of school I had to start looking for a job to pay the bills. I mailed out a few CVs. But I did not specify that I was a total because that would not even get me as far as an interview. I received a call a few days later from a company in Cape Town and I was invited for an interview in the CBD. So I left Durbanville about two hours before the interview to ensure sufficient travelling time. I arrived at Cape Town station about twenty minutes before the interview and made my way through to the Golden Acre. The company was situated on the 22nd floor and I did not even know the Golden Acre had more than five floors. The noise and traffic in town were overwhelming! While navigating around some construction work a *bergie* shouted at me, 'Oubee, oubee, come this side, this is the right side, the other side is suicide.' I was about to cross Adderley Street after waiting about ten minutes for the traffic to calm down when someone suddenly grabbed me from behind, picked me up and carried me across the road. I protested heavily. But this was a big dude and he was not going to put me down for anything. When he put me down on the other side of the road, I thanked him profusely for the embarrassment and took his business card to lodge him at the Dick of the Month club for an award.

I eventually found the correct entrance and a security guard showed me to the lift and I jumped in without any hesitation. I then discovered that the lift had about 50 buttons and well . . . where the . . . was 22? I then pressed all of them, including the emergency alarm and the lift got going. One floor up, stop, another floor up, stop, and Oh my! I lost count. On the next floor I could hear voices so I jumped out and asked for assistance. Finally I managed to find number 22. As I walked into the reception area of the company the receptionist asked me who I was coming to see. I replied that I would love to see Mr Botha, and she told me to take a seat. I asked her where I would find a seat and she replied that I could take any of the fifteen behind me. I then told her it was fine, I'd been sitting since early that morning. After a few minutes she said, 'I see you're a very keen golfer!' And I realised that she was referring to my long cane. I replied that I was a very keen golfer and if Mr Botha did not see me ASAP I'd be late for a 4-ball. Then all of a sudden the penny dropped, and to this day I'm not sure if she was blonde or not. She immediately dragged me off to a chair and ran off to Mr Botha's office and at the top of her voice told him, 'There's a blind guy in reception to see you.' He replied, 'Well, tell him I cannot see him now.' To which I shouted, 'I will never be able to see you and thank God for that!'

There are only a few things that really make my blood boil and one of them is overhanging trees on the pavement that slap me in the face without any warning. Imagine walking with a long cane in the one hand and using the other as a wiper in front of your face. That will look really great or what do you think? I always carry a pair of garden shears in my briefcase to take care of overhanging trees on the routes I use and ensure that no tree slaps me in the face or drips cold water down my back.

I recall being on training in Pretoria during the early nineties and what a blind-friendly city! Most pavements have a paved path running in the centre with grass on both sides and this is great for long cane navigation. After a number of days on course the delegates decided to go out for a few drinks and it ended up being a rather late night. I was travelling to and from the training centre by bus every day and the morning after, I was running a little late. Well, I got on to the bus and within seconds I fell asleep. I woke up a few minutes later and jumped off at my destination. From where I got off it was another four blocks to get to the training centre. I took the first road left, crossed another road and second road left again. At this time I was doing a rather high-speed dash for I was late for my first class.

The next moment I walked slap-bang into a massive tree branch that knocked me off my feet. I could not believe that I had managed to miss this damn thing for the last two weeks. While gathering myself I pulled the garden shears out of my briefcase. It was a rather large bush, but I thought to myself I'd do half now and the rest on my way back that same afternoon. Chik, chik, chik, chik, chik, the branches were flying all over the place. I got about halfway and decided to finish the baby off for I would probably not have time that afternoon. The next moment I heard high heels running in my direction and I was about to ask the woman why she was in such a hurry, when she started to hit me over the head with a broomstick.

'You damn . . . What the . . . are you doing in my garden!' I backed off, but she kept hitting me. Eventually I managed to grab her and the broom and began to explain that I was blind. This, however, pushed her over the edge and she started to scream for help. Needless to say I had taken the wrong turn-off and the bush I was trimming was in the middle of her garden about half a metre away from her front door!

I recall visiting Cape Town on a number of occasions for job interviews and one particular morning while rushing down Shortmarket Street I could hear construction work happening on the opposite side of the road. I was running late and although it was rather noisy I had to push ahead. I managed to pick up my speed after passing the noise and that is the last thing I remember. The next moment I was lying on my back and people were offering me water and I could feel blood running down my face. Believe it or not I'd walked into a massive sign that was covering the entire pavement from left to right and read, 'Mind your head'. The mind boggles!

[*Sound byte*]

I started working for Absa Bank on the switchboard during November 1991 and for the first two months it was fun talking to 800 different people a day. 'Absa Bank, good morning, goeie môre. Absa tot u diens. How can I provide you with excellent service today and for the rest of your life?' I eventually developed multiple personalities to entertain myself. People who knew me would phone in and say who was that nice girl that answered the phone this morning? I would then just laugh and suggest they'd phoned the wrong number.

The switchboard job did get me down and the fact that I allowed it to make me negative unsettled me deeply. I was still single at the time and did not really have someone to share my frustrations with. The only two allies I had at the time were Castle Lager and Cape to Rio Cane. I became more and more negative about life, and began to question God and the universe about why my life was so painfully unfulfilled and boring. One of my total friends, also a switchboard operator, became rather concerned about my well-being, especially one morning after a night out with him and my other two allies when I had got hold of his gun and he literally had to talk me out of the dark side of the moon. [*Enter Bertus and guitar*] He wrote this song for me, called 'Hein's song'. [*Bertus sings 'Hein's Song'. Then exits*]

After working on the bank's switchboard for eighteen months I applied for a job at the Milnerton Municipality, because I thought that people who phone in to complain about their electricity and water being cut off even though their accounts were fully paid-up, would be more interesting. They were indeed! I soon became a self-appointed psychologist and counselled angry ratepayers on how to handle their stress before I transferred them to the appropriate departments. The bank eventually tracked me down and made me a lucrative offer, and before I knew it I was back saying, 'Absa Bank, good morning, goeie môre. How can I provide you with excellent service today and for the rest of your life?'

My passion for computers started when I was still at school. However, this passion almost became an obsession when for the first time I was able to read the front page of the morning newspaper on the Internet. No longer did I have to ask someone else to read me what they thought was important. I could read what I wanted, when I wanted to read it and how I wanted to read it. This made me fall in love with technology. I was 24 years old when I had access to everything and anything I chose to read.

I left the bank and started up my own computer business. I sold computers and software to sighted and non-sighted people. In an attempt to expand my business I started advertising in all the local newspapers; although nowhere in the advert did I specify that this was a blind person selling these computers. That would have been a bad marketing move! After placing another advert in the local Constantia community newspaper I received my first order. 'One computer for my luxury home and one for the office. The one for home use must be more geared for the children's games, etc.' Hmmm, I thought, I'm going to slap you a little with this quotation. The quote was accepted and I rallied up one of our local sixteen-seater-taxi drivers to help me with the delivery of all the computer equipment. If the customer knew this he probably would have cancelled the order immediately.

When I arrived at his home in Constantia, I knocked on the door with my long cane in the one hand and his order form in the other. His wife opened the door, gave me one look and slammed it closed again. I heard her shouting to her husband: 'Honey, there's a blind guy at the door. I think he's collecting for the deaf.' Why do people assume you cannot hear properly if you are blind? After another five minutes she came back to the door and I told her that I was here to deliver and install her husband's computers that he'd ordered from my company. She closed the door again, but this time I'd managed to wangle my long cane into the gap, pushed it open and told her to call her husband immediately. He arrived at the door, gave me a number of dirty looks and told me he would allow me to install the computers if I could tell him 'how on earth a blind man can install computers'. I had to be quick, and I said it had become so easy that you could do it with your eyes closed!

It became rather challenging to continue transporting computer equipment with sixteen-seater taxis in and around Cape Town, and I applied for a job at M-Web's technical call centre. On average I helped 90 sighted people a day to configure their e-mail settings and Internet connection. None of them knew that I could not see. I had to memorise operating systems: Win.95, Win.98, etc. In addition, I had to think in terms of mouse movements, because I do not make use of a computer mouse nor have I ever seen any of the screens. The voice synthesiser gives me a verbal overview of what is on the screen. [*Imitates voice*] 'File, edit, view favourites, tools, help. Microsoft has encountered a problem and your system will be shut down. Please be problem. We have a patient or go to www.thehottestblondes.com.'

After six months at M-Web I became a team leader and managed I.S. (Integrated Systems) technical staff members. They could not understand how I knew when they were lying back in their chairs when helping customers. I'm an expert on body language. Pretty easy. [*Closed voice*] 'Click on tools, then on accounts' versus [*Open voice*] 'click on tools then accounts'.

After another eighteen months I joined Thawte Consulting, the company that made Mark Shuttleworth, the youngster from Durbanville, a billionaire as an IT consultant. When I started at Thawte, the company was growing at a rapid rate and they did not have enough computer screens to give me one. I've been working without one for more than two years and I don't think I'll get one soon. Well, it will take a long time before I can visit those 2-21 websites.

At the age of 22 I exchanged my long cane for my first guide dog, Chelsea – a German shepherd with more soul than most people I've met in my life. We qualified to hit the road after a month of training conducted by the South African Guide-Dogs Association in Johannesburg. When we qualified Chelsea had just turned two years old. She soon knew every pub and hangout around Cape Town and she and her owner were even refused entry to a few of them. Bad publicity took care of most of those.

What still amazes me to this day is the strong bond we developed. If I got up in a certain way she would know we were off to the shop or off to bed or ready to play. She picked it up without me saying anything, purely by my body language. We were connected! We often played mind games with one another, and while I was still working in Cape Town we used to get off the train and race one another through the heavy morning pedestrian traffic in the Golden Acre. Her game was to scare me with the speed with which she navigated our way around obstacles and people, and I always stepped up to the challenge by trying to out-walk her. Oh boy, I miss that dog! I even got her to crap in my manager's office one day.

I did not know that one could have such a close relationship with an animal. She was at my side for seven years, twenty-four hours a day. I remember travelling with her in sixteen-seater taxis and having to pay for three or four people because nobody was prepared to sit next to me. [*Enter Willem with guitar. He plays acoustic*] She fell ill in January 2000 and I had to leave her at home during the day because she could not jump in the car to go to the office any longer. That . . . broke me! My wife, Jill, nursed her until the day she died in her arms. Jill had tried to keep the vet visits and opinions away from me because she knew I wouldn't have been able to handle it. I thank her for her courage. When Chelsea died I asked the vet to send her body for cremation, because I didn't want her to end up on a municipal dumping site. Well, the vet lost her body and to this day I don't know what happened to her remains. [*Exit Willem*]

As a blind person, I've had to hold onto certain thoughts, ideas, call them what you will, to take me through my times of darkness. I've crystallised a few of these. I have always believed that I can. I believe that it is better to be blind and have vision – than to be able to see and have none. I want to leave you with this little story.

Even we blind people sometimes judge a book by its cover. I met up with one of my total friends on Cape Town station late one Friday afternoon to go for a few drinks. Things got going and before we knew it the last train had left the station. The only transport home that we could afford at the time was a sixteen-seater taxi. Eventually we managed to flag one down on Adderley Street. My friend jumped in next to the driver and I worked my way to the sliding door at the back. The door opened and when I stuck my hand in I could feel the taxi was full because it was packed all the way to the door. I jumped on the first person's lap and slammed the door closed. Within seconds we were speeding down the road. The person that I was sitting on kept trying to stick his hands into my pockets and I grabbed his arms and held him down. He protested in isiXhosa, but I did not understand him and the more he protested the more I kept pushing down and holding his arms tightly. When the taxi stopped again to drop people off and pick more people up the guy underneath me forced his way to the door and jumped out. I did not mind because I still had my cellphone and wallet in my pockets. Only then did I realise that he was not trying to steal anything from me, but was rather trying to show me that the rest of the taxi was empty, and I really didn't have to sit on his lap.

Hear you again.

*Curtain call. Hein leads Bertus. Bertus leads Willem. Hein and Bertus turn the wrong way to greet the audience. Willem re-orientates them.*

# A Young Man Living with Epilepsy
*Sithembele Africa Lunguza*

I WAS BUT three years old when I was diagnosed with epilepsy. The stress that this news brought to my family was unbearable since they had to adjust their lives around my health. The financial strain brought about by this condition was as palpable as our poverty and our lack of resources spoke volumes.

I am now 33 years old and managing the Office on the Status of Disabled Persons (OSDP) in the Eastern Cape Provincial Government. My work is centred around empowering government departments to progressively implement legislation that ensures the interests of people with disabilities are catered for. Prior to taking up my present position I was a Deputy Director in the Office of the Premier in the North West Province, managing the OSPD in the Special Programmes Directorate. And before that, I was Deputy Director at the Department of Social Development in Mpumalanga, where I managed the Social Research and Policy Monitoring Unit.

Growing up was not a walk in the park for an epileptic young man. 'Epileptic' was a label used to keep me from enjoying social amenities and other inalienable benefits. Degradation, dehumanisation and humiliation by my peers prompted suicidal tendencies as I began to hate myself. Promises about a rosy tomorrow paralysed my hopes for a better future. I began to internalise the humiliating speeches of my peers as I succumbed to their teasing. This whole fiasco negatively affected my self-esteem, and

I began to hide in the shadows. At school I was made the centre of attraction as teachers mocked my condition whenever I made a mistake. My peers were advised to shun me because of my 'contagious condition'. They believed that I would bite them during one of my seizures.

Epilepsy is superstitiously viewed as a sickness that emanates from witchcraft. It is believed that witches have got powers to cast spells that can cause epilepsy. It is also believed that traditional healers have medicine to defeat the demonic powers and to cure epilepsy. People believe this because in some cases those who had consulted traditional healers had been healed and stopped having seizures. This mindset affected the thinking of my family, because several traditional healers were consulted, and in the process, huge sums of money were paid out. But to no avail.

Since my family had no resources to access private medical facilities, there was no choice for me but to attend a public hospital for treatment to control my seizures. I was traumatised by the long queues, the arrogant nursing staff and the spectacle of fragile patients who were in desperate need of medical attention. At hospitals we were spoken to as if we were psychotic. This apparent lack of empathy stems directly from an inadequate understanding of epilepsy and from the various myths surrounding the condition. For example, it is believed that this condition is contagious, even though there is no scientific evidence whatsoever to back this claim.

As I was growing up, my social relations were soured by my condition and I ended up separating myself from my age group. My schooling days were tantamount to hell as my peers avoided me like an abomination. No one wanted to sit next to me, because they believed that my burp would infect them. In a society where ignorance is the norm, even those whom I thought possessed some knowledge (the teachers) never bothered to educate others about my disability.

All of this led to changes in my behaviour. I remember vividly how I used to dodge classes in primary school, beating up my peers, being reserved, stealing, and roaming the streets with friends until dawn. This affected my family terribly, in particular my mother who had to leave work and plead my case to the principal. The principal of Seyisi Lower Primary School at the time was Mrs Mdingi, who was indeed very fond of me and protected me against the odds. However, I did not escape her cane every time I dodged classes. Unaware at the time that she was building character in me, I kept on dodging lessons. It was the intervention of my aunt, Nokwakha Jelu, in my unbecoming behaviour that was the turning point. She was generally regarded as the 'iron lady' who did not take any nonsense. I attribute my change of behaviour to her, as she would take me to school by the hand and wait for me to go straight home afterwards to clean or undertake the other chores that I thought were meant for girls, such as cooking. Today, I am an all-rounder, thanks to her.

When I went to university, I became active in politics. In 1998 I was the Transformation Officer of the South African Student Congress (SASCO), a student political movement. In the subsequent year, I was elected as the Transformation Officer in the Student Representative Council (SRC). This helped me to discover my leadership capabilities and restore my self-esteem. Public presentations and meetings with highly esteemed personalities boosted and re-energised my confidence. It was during these days that I realised a need for services for people with epilepsy in the Eastern Cape Province. I engaged with the then South African National Epilepsy League (SANEL), now Epilepsy South Africa, and shared my vision with the management. Kathy Pahl and Anthony Pascoe flew down to Grahamstown to listen to my proposal. With the assistance of Epilepsy South Africa's management, I assembled a group of passionate students to instigate and raise awareness on issues of epilepsy. The name of the group was the Grahamstown Epilepsy Support Group. This group made an impact at the university by raising awareness. We were invited to several radio talk shows to explain our plight. The members of the group were also empowered to understand the multi-faceted issues surrounding disability.

Through the courtesy of Epilepsy South Africa, I was later introduced to Disabled People South Africa (DPSA) where I became a mouthpiece for people living with disabilities. I worked for DPSA in the Eastern Cape Province and my responsibilities in the organisation included research and policy advocacy activities. Through my stay at DPSA from October 2001 to November 2003 I became empowered and contributed by creating a positive image about disability. However, it did pose some challenges as some of my colleagues perceived me as an outsider. This was caused by a very narrow understanding of disability which centred only around physical features of disability, for example, paraplegia. This experience still haunts me. However, I view it as a challenge now and see in it a need to educate my society.

It is evident that regardless of our disabilities, if given opportunities we can achieve wonders in life. Indeed, there is no limit to what a person can do because I believe one sets one's own limits. I believe you are your own asset and there is nothing you cannot do if you believe in it. I trust that if God brings you to something, then He will bring you through it. Looking back on my life, I am a living example of this. I matriculated from Ndzondelelo High School in 1996 and joined Rhodes University in 1997. In 2000 I graduated with a Bachelor of Social Sciences and a Postgraduate Diploma in International Studies. In 2001 I obtained a Certificate in International Conflict Studies from Uppsala University in Sweden. I am currently pursuing Project Management with Intec College. I am also seriously considering pursuing a Masters Programme in Disability Management with the University of Cape Town or the Masters Programme in Public Policy Management with Wits University. What keeps me going is the urge to make a difference by adding value to our new democracy. As the tide turns, it is fitting that we be found ready with the relevant skills.

Who would have thought that I would ever be where I am today? This clearly attests to my claim that God has a purpose for every one of us. For all those who have enhanced my life for the better, I am fraternally grateful.

# Taking a Break
### *Kevin Dean Hollinshead*

Brains are longing for leave
A well-earned sabbatical
No clue as to
Where you might find them
But have a look
In the pot-plants

She says there's
More than free space
Between these ears
High-quality neurons in fact
Just wish there were more
Could argue but who really cares that much anyway.

# My Own Experiences
*Barbara Watt*

I HAD A GUN accident when I was three years old. Through this, my spinal cord was damaged and I became paralysed from the waist down. The doctor told my parents that it would have been better if I had died! The doctor knew how difficult it would be growing up with a disability; but, like so many people, he probably viewed people with disabilities as useless, having no purpose and being a burden to society.

I will always be thankful that my parents treated me the same as my sister, with the same discipline, and gave me the same opportunities as her. But as I grew up I found that others treated me differently – they stared, pointed, talked about me. Children at school can be very cruel to one another, especially to anyone who is different. The one who is different is generally rejected and this is very hurtful. I also often heard those words, 'Ag Shame!' But I didn't want pity, I wanted acceptance.

One day we went on holiday. I was about fourteen years old and as I sat in my wheelchair, outside the holiday home, waiting for my parents, a man came along and gave me twenty cents. I was so disgusted – did he think I was a beggar or a 'cripple' (as they called them in the Bible) sitting on the street?

When others treat you differently or do not accept you, this determines the way you view yourself, especially if this happens as you are growing up. You develop a negative self-image, as well as feelings of rejection and of worthlessness.

My teenage years were very difficult – no boys were interested in me. But then I learnt that I needed to be friendly first, to help others accept me. I could choose to be a bitter or a better person because of my difficulties. The biggest healing was when I realised that God accepts me and loves me just as I am. It is Jesus Christ who gives my life meaning and purpose.

'Is it accessible?' Every person with a disability knows what this means. Freedom of movement is most important for a disabled person. Some people say I am 'confined' to my wheelchair, but my wheelchair gives me freedom to move around. It is the environment that inhibits my freedom of movement. Obviously, I cannot apply for employment which is up a flight of stairs or where the toilets are too small for my wheelchair. Wherever I go I need to consider whether it is going to be accessible for my wheelchair. Most able-bodied people are not even aware that they are walking up a flight of stairs or stepping over something in their way.

Over many years, I was involved in various Access Committees, endeavouring to make the environment more friendly to people with disabilities. My theme was: 'Where a wheelchair can go, anyone can go!' When faced with a flight of stairs at a public place, I have often been told to 'go around the back'. In a way, I have faced discrimination just as so many people did during apartheid.

Schools and other educational institutions, especially, need to be accessible. In certain cases I believe there should be special schools for children with disabilities, but generally schools need to include everyone. When my daughter started school, it was important for me to be able to get to her classroom, to the hall and the headmaster's office. It's not only important for the scholar who is disabled, but also for the mother who is disabled.

In fact every aspect of a wheelchaired person's life is affected by accessibility, whether it be housing, work, transport, hospitals, churches or social life. Most people with spinal cord injuries have paralysed bladders and bowels, so having an accessible toilet wherever the person goes is important. One day a friend phoned me and told me how excited he was that the church he attended had put in an accessible toilet. No longer did he need to be concerned that he would have 'an accident' if the service went on too long and he could not get home in time. How strange that two people could have such an excited discussion about a toilet.

Thinking about wheelchairs and accessibility, two incidents come to mind. Firstly, there is nineteen-year-old Wanda. He lived in a rural area and longed to work, like his brothers and sisters. The taxis did not want to transport him in his wheelchair, and if they did, it would be at an exorbitant price. Wanda so desperately wanted to get to the workshop. One day I was talking to the director of a residential home for people with disabilities. A bed had just become available. And so it was that Wanda moved in and was able to start work at the workshop, where many disabled people did contracts for various companies. A group of the youngsters was also taken on holiday to the beach. Wanda was so excited. He had never seen the sea before and jumped (as it were) out of his wheelchair to get to the seawater. His whole life had changed.

Then there was John, who one day was carefully manoeuvring his wheelchair off the pavement by holding onto the parking meter – there was no ramp close by. Just then a man came along, grabbed onto the wheelchair handles and picked him up, putting him straight back onto the pavement! 'There you are,' the man said and walked off. The man was only trying to help, but poor John had to start to get off the pavement all over again. We all roared with laughter when he told us the story. It is very helpful to have a sense of humour when disabled!

It would seem that many South Africans would like to park right in the shopping centre itself, if they could, because they are too lazy to walk from the car park. It is absolutely shocking to see the continual abuse of the parking bays especially set aside for people with disabilities. These parking bays are wider than the norm, to give extra space for a wheelchair when getting in and out of a car. They are also situated close to the front door of the shopping centre to reduce the distance of pushing a wheelchair. It is an uphill battle to find a parking place that is not occupied by someone who is not disabled, whose usual comment, when challenged, is: 'Oh, I'm just going to be a few minutes!'

There is the joke about the little boy who said to his mother: 'Mummy, why are those cars parked there? I thought they were meant for wheelchairs!'

Yes, it is important to have accessibility to buildings. But perhaps the greatest need is to have changed attitudes and to get rid of prejudice. When this happens, then people will understand and are more likely to put in ramps and to consider the special needs of the disabled before any building is even constructed.

Despite all the prejudices and difficulties I have faced in my life, I am thankful to God and my encouraging parents. Although I have had many medical problems, I have lived a full life and been blessed with so much: a husband of fifteen years, a lovely daughter who lives overseas, and many good friends. It was wonderful to travel overseas and to represent KwaZulu-Natal twice at sport for the disabled. I also own my own home and have a fulfilling job.

Having the right attitude to disabled people can make a difference, wherever you go or work. You can speak up when you see prejudice against disabled people or if you are aware of any environment where disabled people are not considered – especially when parking places are abused!

# Three Beautiful Senses
*Zohra Moosa*

You hear the doorbell
I see the flashing lamp
You hear the words over the telephone
I watch the words on the screen
You hear human voices
I watch the interpreter's sign
You hear the joyous greetings
I feel the friendly hands
You hear the sound of laughter
I see a joyous smile
You hear the anger in a voice
I see the awful expression

You hear the howling of wind
I watch the leaves swaying and falling
You hear the stormy night
I watch the heavy downpour with lightning
You hear the angry wild waves
I watch the frothy water break against a rock
You hear the melody of music
I feel the catchy beat

You hear the cheerful chirping birds
I watch them flying gracefully

You hear
the words
the sounds of nature
of human voices

I see the expressions
I feel the sounds
I watch the actions
I see
I feel
I watch.

# When I Walk . . .
*Mak Manaka*

The sun will scorch the earth
Unwanted infants will cry before birth
Believers in humanity
Will live after death
And taste their spiritual wealth
When feelings in my toes
Can tell the difference
Between solid ground and carpets
The moon will commit adultery
With the beautiful evening star
And father my daughter.
On that day
Rain will pour heavily
Yet children will play
And those who are unable to speak
Will have a say

When I walk
The deaf will talk
The blind will stare
And hope to live another day to share
The images they saw the past year

Hatred will cease
Violence will be an illusive breeze
And all this abuse will have to freeze,
Eternally
Coz respect for one's self
Must manifest even toward the elderly

Without my two boys
I wonder if I will still make noise
When life's liquid begins to ooze
A fresh breath of air through my bones
There will be an end
To bloodshed

The world has seen and will continue to see
A million me's
Planting nations
As strong as Samson's DNA
Coz when I walk
Unborn prophets will listen
To poets spit lines to the sun
Even after dawn

Babies will speak before they teethe
This is not deep
But understand before YOU believe
That when I walk
My mother's eyes will spark

In the dark
And give life to feelings
Murdered by the past

So until that day comes
Let's hold on to our dreams.

# A Blind Man and his Guitar
## *Mlungisi Khumalo*

Hurrying feet passing by,
The strings of a talking guitar
Are swallowed into the noise of the street
The hooting cars and the shouting hawkers
And the more visible activity of town

A young boy in red shorts
Would sometimes dance on the side
Protruding toes doing the magic,
A leader a dancer and a collector of pennies

I pass by
Sometimes quicker than I like to
Or than my legs can afford
And I leave only my ear behind
I love the music – it's getting into me,
But how can I stop,
A crippled man on crutches
Watching a blind man in glasses,
This is weird
So would the passers-by observe

On occasions I dream of him
At night in the quiet of my room

I love what I hear
I'll pass by tomorrow
And probably the day after tomorrow.

'A Quiet Time' – Musa Zulu

# Shelter

*Kobus Moolman*

THERE ARE TWO bus shelters just around the corner from where he lives in Greyling Street – from the house he has always lived in. One shelter he likes and uses most of the time; mainly to wait for the Saturday morning bus to take him to town, to the children's library in the centre of town, or to the OK Bazaars to buy himself a Lucky Packet (in the shape of a small, brightly-coloured cardboard suitcase) with money he received for his birthday, or to King's Sports to look at their bats or to get another tennis ball after his was confiscated by the woman next door for damaging her flowers during a cricket match between his brother and himself.

The other bus shelter – the one he does not like – is probably closer, but he does not use it. He is not able to walk long distances, so it would make sense to use this one. But he does not. He cannot even remember ever having used it, although he knows that he must have done at some point (or driven past it with his parents), for how else would he have known that he does not like it?

Sometimes he thinks it is because his favourite shelter is situated along the exact road he walks to school every week from Monday to Friday (excepting for school holidays). If this is true – and already he knows enough about himself to suspect so – then he feels just a little afraid, for it would mean that he is a creature of habit; that he is, in fact, already laying down on a daily basis a pattern of living he might come to regret at some point in his future. But the future is too far away for him to be concerned. He is nine years old and he cannot see any reason why he should not remain nine for the rest of his life.

His favourite bus shelter is made of tin. It is closed on three sides and has a roof that sticks out like the peak of a cap. The seat is not solid but consists of two polished wooden strips. When he sits he can swing his legs vigorously, and his feet do not scrape the pavement. There is a pole painted yellow just in front of the shelter – in fact, it stands between the shelter and the edge of the road. There is a small sign on the top of the pole with a number on it, but he does not remember ever taking notice of it. He waits always for the bus with 'City/Stad' displayed in black capital letters on the front. When he returns from town, from his solitary shopping expedition, he looks for the bus marked 'Clarendon'. He does not live in this fancy suburb on the hill – his father is a storeman in a chocolate factory – but the bus that goes there has to drive through a section of the lower end of town where he lives.

He is not yet conscious of any difference in his life as a result of living in a street where people have names like Koekie and Poppie and the Eyetie, and where they fix their cars in the front garden, or in the road because they don't have a garden at all. However, he is aware that there is something different about him because of the way people look at him when he climbs onto the bus or walks into a shop, and then he understands why his mother fusses over him so much and why he is not part of any of the gangs at school. He is not sure but he suspects that another reason he likes this small tin bus shelter is because he cannot be seen once he is inside and he has drawn his legs up onto the seat beside him like a pair of crutches. This desire to hide himself away is perhaps yet another pattern he realises that he is building for himself, from which he will not be able to escape. But he does not know what else a small boy can do who is not able to run or jump or play team sports like other children. The other children do not want him on their team. He is too slow. He falls over when they pass the ball to him. He wets himself from anxiety.

He was included once, though. In a football match between the boys and the girls. When he played goalie for the girls. He saved a goal on that occasion, and all the girls jumped up and down and screamed and put their arms around him, and one girl even kissed him on the cheek, twice – a small girl with freckles on her face and a pale skin and sad mouth that was always turned down. They still lost 7-0 though.

On another occasion, an occasion of which he is extraordinarily proud, he won the Dressing-Up Race at school. This was the first and the only race he has ever won in his short life. In the race the boys had to run to a large heap of clothing piled up in the middle of the field which they had brought from the wardrobe of their big sister or their mother. (This part of the race he naturally lost.) Dresses, shoes, hats and handbags were all jumbled together and the boys first had to scrabble and scratch around to find all of their mother's or older sister's items. Then they had to get dressed as quickly as they could – dropping the awkward frocks over their small shoulders – and, hitching up their trailing skirts, run slide-shuffling in oversize shoes to the finish line at the end of the field. He won this part of the race hands down. His favourite game at home is to dress up in his older sister's outfits and parade around the house talking to himself as if he were some high-society lady. He knows how to do up buttons and zips; how to slide-shuffle in his mother's shoes that fit snugly over his small, black orthopaedic boots. 'Stop that!' his mother would always shout at him. 'You're stretching my shoes.' But she never took her shoes away.

His prize for winning the race that day was an inflatable figure of a clown that stood upright once its bottom had been weighted with water. It was virtually impossible then to knock the smiling plastic man over. No matter how hard he punched or kicked it the clown would simply bounce straight back up again. Down and up, down and up the little figure would go all day long, no matter how hard he hit it. Down and straight back up again. Down and straight back up again. He thinks that this is a very good description of how he walks too. He tells himself that at least he knows how to fall without hurting himself.

There are two ways he can walk to get to the small tin shelter to catch the 'City/Stad' bus. When he comes out of his green front gate he can either walk all the way down Greyling Street until he comes to Oxford Street, turn right at the house with the knobbly walls, walk straight up this street with its crooked and uneven paving blocks, turn left at the bottom into Boom Street, past the little café on the corner, and on to the bus shelter a hundred metres or so below. This is the one way. What he calls the Long Way. Though by normal standards it is not long at all.

Or he can take the short route. In actuality, it is probably not much shorter (if at all), and really only involves cutting out the greater part of Boom Street by taking a tiny lane (Stead Lane) that sneaks behind the unkempt backyards of the same houses that front onto the Long Way. It is, however, the more interesting route. At least for a boy who enjoys tales of the weird and wonderful. For, apart from the overgrown backyards with their rusty corrugated iron fences and scraggly fruit trees, the Short Way has the attraction of two strange creatures. Again, not strange by normal standards. But strange enough for someone who has spent his entire life in one street in the lower end of the city.

The first creature is a white goose. It makes him think of 'The Snow Goose'. But this bird from Stead Lane is definitely not the same idea of unwavering affection that the Snow Goose is in the story he likes to listen to on his sister's record. It hisses like a snake and twists its long neck about just like a snake when he walks down the lane. Because he knows that it cannot get through the wire fence (its wings have also been clipped, his father assures him) he sometimes stands for a long time enjoying the terrifying thrill of danger while the large bird with wings outstretched sways and jabs at the air between them.

But two houses down from the goose is an almost opposite creature. And one of which he is more genuinely afraid since it seems never to notice him, has never made a sound as far as he can remember, and is content simply to stand staring fixedly at him like a mythic beast from one of the books on legends that he always takes out of the library. It is a tall, elegant bird. A blue crane. Rescued perhaps from the side of some rural road where it lay flapping its broken mauve wing helplessly. He does not know for sure. Whatever its origin, he has never seen it move, but knows it is alive only because it is never in the same place in the garden. He does not look at it for long, afraid that, like the Medusa, it will turn its victims to stone.

There is one problem, however, with this short cut, which, despite the dangerous and exotic attraction of the birds, causes him more often than not to avoid it. For the end of Stead Lane, where it leads back into the top part of Boom Street, is a dirt track overgrown on the sides with wild banana trees and bushes that never flower but give off a putrefying smell from their leaves. The track is also often covered in rubbish. It is a path that he always regrets having to go down, that makes him wish he had never chosen to walk down the lane to look at the two birds, that he had suffered instead the narrow pavement of Boom Street, where the uneven blocks threaten at every step to pitch him into the deep gutters.

He tells no one of his fears and his secret thrills. He closes himself off from admitting the truth to anyone as if he himself were a book that he could simply shut and forget. (But how many stories are there which he does in fact forget?) It is a strategy he cannot ever remember learning, but seems to have been born with. As he was born with stupid feet and a hole at the base of his spine. As he was born with soft brown eyes.

Once again he has an intimation that some dark pattern of behaviour is being worn into his being that, once established, he will find difficult to free himself from. But he does not know how else to survive. It is not a choice. It is simply what he has to do in order to win other dressing-up races. In order not to wet himself with anxiety when a playmate passes the ball to him, shouting, 'Score! Score! It's wide open!'

And he falls.

★ ★ ★

But then there is the case of the other bus shelter. The one he does not use. It, too, is only just around the corner from where he lives. Like his favourite shelter. But at the opposite end of that same road. And there is only one way to get to it. There is no short cut.

To get to it he has to come out of his small front gate and walk up Greyling Street, rather than down, as if he were going to his favourite shelter. At the corner of Greyling and West streets he turns left and walks up West until he gets to Boom Street. And there, barely a few metres from the corner, is the second bus shelter, that he cannot remember ever having used. He just does not like the way it looks. It is a large, old, wooden structure painted dark green, municipal green. It is open on both sides. The shelter takes up the whole width of the pavement so that pedestrians walk straight through it all the time. It has a long wooden roof. And on rainy days it is difficult to tell legitimate commuters from those who are simply taking temporary shelter from the storm.

The ground in front of the shelter – between the end of the pavement and the edge of the road – is in the shade of large jacaranda trees, and is treacherous in summer. In general, he is very fond of trees. He likes to climb the thick branches of the plum tree that stands at the bottom of his garden, and pretend to be a pirate on the rigging of a swaying sailing ship.

But in summer the ground under these jacarandas is muddy and churned up by the continual traffic of feet. And the purple flowers of the tree that lie squashed on the wet earth are as slippery as ice to his unbalanced step.

He wonders how he knows this to be so if, as he claims, he has never used this bus shelter. Perhaps it is not only a weak back and crooked legs that he suffers from, but also a faulty memory. Perhaps he has visited this green bus shelter on several occasions, and disliked it each time (perhaps it is the feeling of being exposed that puts him off), and each time purposefully removed it from his memory. Perhaps he visits it in his dreams. The dreams he also cannot remember.

How will he find out? Know for sure that he does not just make up details and events in his life, the same way he makes up stories to help him go to sleep at night? How will he know if there is ever anything real in his life? Or if it is all simply a small chapter in a book he has forgotten to return to the library. A book that lies under his bed gathering dust and dreams.

He is ready. He is dressed for the trip. He wears his purple, plastic GI helmet with the broken strap for protection. He wears his favourite green zip-up corduroy jacket for luck. He walks slowly. Not that he is afraid. But he wants to be sure that he remembers everything. He also wants to find out if there is not some small detail on the way – a rusty back gate that creaks in a particular way, a bush in flower, the trilling of flightless birds in a cage – that will set off the certainty of recognition in him, and finally put to rest the mystery of the wooden bus shelter.

That is where the Bothas live. In that corrugated iron house with the rickety wooden fence and the small outside toilet. They have two sons. The one is a one-eyed postman who sits around in his uniform when he is not working. The other spends most of his time fishing with his scrawny friends who've been in jail (or so his father tells him) and who drink heavily. Their whole family is sullen and uncommunicative. On the side of the house, under the roof, is a collection of long planks and poles that Mr Botha is saving for something. But no one knows what. Mrs Botha makes delicious fish cakes which she sometimes gives to the boy's mother on a plate covered with an old dishcloth. He eats them still hot, and they burn the tips of his fingers.

And there is the Nels' house. The big house with the large empty yard in the front. He has seldom seen anyone from their family, except their Ouma, who is a small busy-body and walks with quick steps like a nervous bird. She is old and always looks irritated. Every day she hurries past his house to visit her friend who lives down the road. Next door to the Nels is a house with a beautiful yesterday-today-and-tomorrow bush right at the front gate. He stops. It is one of his favourite smells. That and the warm smell of chocolate that comes wafting on the air from his father's factory some blocks away, on a summer's evening when it stays light late and he can play outside longer, building roads in the soil of his Oupa's vegetable garden or bowling coolie-creepers and spinners and googlies to his brother behind their father's shed. He taps on his plastic helmet to bring himself back from his daydream.

But then a funny thing begins to happen to him as he walks. It is not so much the past that comes back to him as he had hoped (in overwhelming bursts of renewal). Rather, it is the fullness of the moment he is standing in that expands and keeps expanding like a balloon beneath his senses; deepening itself like the night-sky that he often looks up at from his front verandah step, stretching further and further away from his imagination the more he tries to put a limit to it. And so the yesterday-today-and-tomorrow bush takes on the smell of chocolate on a warm evening, and the smell of chocolate is the smell of freshly cut grass lying out at the back waiting for him to rake it together, and the smell of the grass is the smell of his mother's hands when she rubs his legs with Deep Heat after a bath. And so on. And more. Until he is full and bursting. Until the present is so big that he knows all the books in the children's library in town will not ever be able to contain it. He is dizzy. He is dizzy. He is about to fall over. Where is he? How did he get here? To the green wooden bus shelter on the corner of Boom and West streets.

And there is an orange corporation bus waiting for him. It is the 'City/Stad' bus. It is empty. He can sit wherever he likes. He can have the long back seat all to himself.

'Hello,' says Charlie the driver. 'Are you going to town? Are you going to the library?' The ticket in the boy's hand is green, and slightly damp from holding it so tightly. The ground between him and the bus is dry. He can walk across it easily.

'Have you changed bus stops?' says Charlie. 'Are you breaking out at last?'

And the boy in the plastic helmet smiles. He holds out his ticket, and smiles.

# Somebody to Whisper
## *Looks Matoto*

my old time craving
somebody help i'm starving
just to hear one comrade so true
that will be the only jewel left of my
country
many comrades turned hypocrites
some to blood-sucking parasites
can somebody whisper me freedom

there shall be houses, security
and comfort
forward we shall march to a
people's government
these songs we knew by heart
how sad to see them fade fast
is there any comrade left
just to whisper me freedom

i shall not be confused
i can never be used
my comrades have forgotten freedom
they each strive for stardom

many turned to politricks
to be rich you have to pull your tricks
is there anyone left to whisper me
freedom

my country filled with walking shells
prisoners of loans and debts
they live and rely on credit
black is listed on credit bureaus
somebody whisper me freedom

they walk the street with exaggerated smiles
just to hide their deep enrooted pain
they walk with letters of the sheriff in
hand
houses and furniture attached
poverty on the white linen of freedom
is a stain
please can somebody help
whisper me freedom

my colour dominates the airwaves still
fed to lions alive
dragged on the streets by ropes tied to
cars
whilst the white party goes on
when i talk these truths

the other colour labels it hate speech
please somebody whisper me freedom

the house of truth is filled with vandalism
whilst honourable men walk in and out of
the houses of lies
there is only one colour that burns
pitch black in the shark houses
the only colour you will find in
RDP houses
constantly wiped away by floods
oh any comrade left to whisper
me freedom.

# New Prison
*Sipho Mkhize*

The New Prison of Apartheid
from where the blood flowed like
water flowing in the river, even
the Orange River itself won't be big enough
to accommodate all the bloodshed
of the New Prison.
The year 1993 was the year of dancing
on our blood.
November 20, I won't forget you,
we were dancing on our blood, yes,
I still remember that day
the day of November 20.
The blood of our fellow prisoners was running
from the fourth floor to the first floor.
We heard the sound of home-made instruments,
instruments of gangsterism.
A New Prison of Apartheid
down the valley of Maritzburg
at the cemeteries of the Boers.
I believe that it was in revenge for King Dingane.

I believe that they remind me of the killing
of Steve Bantu Biko.
And I warn you that this country is not for revenge,
slavery and bloodshed.
God gave us a life
but the New Prison takes it away.

# In Memory of a Friend
*Piwe Mkhize*

And oh,
The earth remains quiet after
We have buried our loved ones,
The pieces of soil cover them,
Love them,
Embrace them,
And complete nothingness prevails,
And like the wind wiping the earth of its dirt,
The HIV/AIDS virus is here, next door,
And perhaps in my own bloodstream,
Still distilling the beauty we have known –
They are now gone,
Peacefully, eternally.

# Robben Island
*Giulio Scapin*

There is an island
at the southern point of Africa
where Christian and Muslim
the healthy and the sick
African and European
Jew as well as Asian
lived together in exile
for their beloved country
SOUTH AFRICA!

# We are Alive
## *Mak Manaka*

10 years before today
This moment
Was still a dream,
And so my time and your time
Is not before or after but NOW

I refuse to sleep
In a bed
Coloured in race and gender conflicts
Coz 10 years before this time
Our fathers wrote history on our palms
So we could read and learn from our past
Yet we painted our destiny
With crippled brush strokes
Of liberation
And saw the sun
Call for rain.

Before now
We were ripples of discrimination
A repetition
Of silent pain

We died a million times
Before the 'X'
Marked a black president.
We were patriots of understanding
And victims of shame
Long before they called us cripples.

And here we stand
In the centre of attention
Proclaiming our dreams
With open hearts.
We walk free
From names like:
>   Disabled,
>     Isidalwa,
>        Sekgwele

10 years after now
My children will live with stars
Of an open-minded galaxy
They will remember this moment
For this time is legendary
What happens now
Shapes and saves
Future perceptions of our selves.

Coz 10 years from now
I don't want to see myself

As a struggling writer
Hustling and juggling words
To provide for a family
And so change and expand
Are my biggest priorities
Hold on to your dreams
Coz your time is NOW!

# Texture of a Dream
*Motsoakgomo 'Papi' Nkoli*

My fingertips reach out
and I touch . . .
a wonder, I think it is.
Tenderly vivid episodes of eruptions and floods
soak my eyeballs.

Indelible roots grow from my face
and clasp me into the scenic labyrinth of disappearance.
Very real it is.
Indeed beautiful!

I still say . . .

My pulse-rhythms wrestle with disbelief.
Leakages of realisations born:
and I, a purist of a sentient voodoo,
am hypnotised into a trance of
elephantine candle-wax dancing,
and the immortal harmonious smells falling from
the full moon.

The gallery of colours I travel in dangles and floats,
leaving me mumbling distant tongues that sail me
in a bubble.

A piece of a dream I eat,
for its taste may change the next time I dream.
Once more?
Will I ever dream?

The rarity and remoteness in this airy mood
blows textures of the dream to my fingers
and plants them inside the enigmatic human conviction.

See this simplicity in the eyes?
It is the glass fence
shielding my foam-baked dreams
lest they dissolve in the vogue.

The burning sweetness of love
happily whirls under this fragile skin of mine,
leaving my heart empty
like an amor-maniac.

How does it feel now?

# A Poet's Life
*Piwe Mkhize*

I like a poet's life
I dream a poet's dream
I may be a poet
Who said poets are lonely people . . .?
Who said poets had inadequacies . . .?
Why are rolling summer mountain
Ranges lonely until they encounter
A human eye . . .?
Why do memories of men and women
Find their museum in poetry . . .?
Why do lovers love a writer's literature . . .?
Who is not a storyteller . . .?
Who said writers don't love . . .?
Who said poets are lonely people . . .?
I am a poet.
I live a lonely poet's life
And I have lots of love —
Unclaimed.
I do dream a poet's dream,
I am a real poet,
All poets have one thing to give,
The pouring present of their

Wide world of words,
Poets are people, real people,
Poets want to fall in love
Poets do fall in love.
So I am a poet,
I am forever in love with many
A potential love
I am poetry
Poetry can only be as
Contradictory and controversial as my life,
Poetry mirrors life's intricacies
And complexities.
I like a poet's life,
My life is poetry at its worst.

# Word of Mouth
## *Jillian Hamilton*

gobble books for breakfast
devour books for dinner
licking the gravy from the pages
chew great forksful
in a midnight feast
bite, gnaw, gulp, swallow
grow plump with the words
replete with line after line
of sweet inspiration
until you belch
and sigh
and must sleep
for digestion's sake

erect a monument to the Word
a tower to the sky
of mayan tablets
papyrus rolled in hieroglyphs
the book of changes

pile gutenberg's bible
upon gilt-edged manuscripts

scribed by monks
tomes, soft covered
slim volumes
bound in calfskin leather
banned books
bad books
and balanced on the top
head in the heavens
the Writer
i grow hungry...
a book!
a book!

# Gazing at the Drop
## *Mlungisi Khumalo*

After a heavy rainfall
The night is quietened down
At midnight I'm writing my poetry
Gazing at the drop . . .
Hanging from the rust of my roof
My old roof, my shelter, my world
It is trivial in the dim light of my candle
My eye catches it – sticks to it
Diminished in the wink of an eye . . .
It drops with splendour onto my table
Expands to greatness and pride . . .
The cock crows
The night is over
My work is done . . .

# Limpopo Village

*Kobus Moolman*

(from *Separating the Seas*)

– The dirt road is
dry, entirely red
and dry.

– The sky is empty
all the way from
one end to the other.

– A brindled cow
comes down the dirt road
ringing a cracked bell.

– Red clay pots lie
broken on both sides
of the red road.

– A white chicken squawks
under the arm
of a young girl.

– On her head the girl carries
her old wooden bed
to her wedding.

# Chirara

*Kevin Dean Hollinshead*

(Chirara is a campsite on the eastern shores of
Lake Kariba, Zimbabwe)

A fish eagle cry
To pierce the vacant air
Scorching heat, paper thorns
And leafless Baobabs
An arid riverbed
Where elephant roam
Dry, hot earth
Under a young boy's feet
Brittle grass, bleached by the sun.

'Taking the Wood Home' – William Zulu

# A Sizzling Heart

*Zanele Dolly Simelane*

A burning heart sizzles like a fragmented dream
This heart knows no mercy to its inflictor
The pumping of this heart knows not how to whisper
Its hopes and desires

This sizzling heart bares scars forgotten
At the appearance of its capturer
This heart, heavy with seduction and lust
Heart shaped like a blob that fills the throat waiting to lament
This heart bears forgiveness and deceit

Heart full of love, heart full of desire for a dream
Never been realised by its bearer and predecessors
This heart full of warmth and malice
Heart made of steel yet that breaks with every tinkle of unfaithfulness

The heart that is congested with plagues of longing
This heart awaits a perfect fit
This heart is broken by them, it and those
This heart longs to love and be loved

This heart inflicts pain on itself
Whenever it opens up to me, you and them
A heart brimming with rage
A heart withering with sorrow

This heart, the one I gave and give and will give
The heart I pierce with tales of love and loss.

# For the Sake of the Struggle!
*Sipho Mkhize*

Oh, yes, girl of Bhungane!
Of course, Queen of Makhulunkhulu,
to you, Roman Catholic volunteer, that was for the sake of the struggle,
I left my love deep in the heart of an angel,
an angel who clapped her wings at the first stop of Dambuza;
the evidence of God was her smile, to make the sun rise;
the time of religion and love was like a thumb going to tobacco.
We prayed for our everlasting love,
we took friends and love as an unremoved mountain.
Now I'm here too far from you, for the sake of the struggle.

During those days, Dambuza Road became
boiling mud, street lights went suddenly off;
All youths blew their whistles; next to the corners
guns were sounding like thunder; that was for the
sake of struggle, the days of Operation Clean Up.
It was my duty to turn Dambuza Road into a good condition.
I was injured, I lost my leg, I contributed with my leg.
Now I don't see any shade of you,
I don't see you, my love. I'm in
the darkest place, for the sake of the struggle, darling.

# The Apple
*Jacqui Edwards*

Eating the clean inside of this apple
The seeds dropping from my lips
    Where did it all go?
I am left with this dark stalk
    I discard that.

# Matchgirl

*Shelley Barry*

Searching for pieces of fire
Flames turn to smoke

Again and again
Her feet scratch the surface
Looking for some corridor to him

He holds out dead flowers –
His bouquet of truth

No utterance from him
Will turn his mouth into a flame
Where she can bake her heart.

# Food
*Jacqui Edwards*

Filling my belly
Stuffing my birthday cake into a sad face
The insufficiency of the rich cream and chocolate crumbles
Left, wanting to vomit
This love-sick stomach out.

# Snap
*Jacqui Edwards*

I am broken –
Into shape!

# On My 40th

*Kevin Dean Hollinshead*

It's wonderful to be
As decrepit as me!
Girls galore
And perks abound . . .
Guests unlimited –
I'm 40 today . . .
I'll celebrate life
In my no-comment way!

# Reality Check
### *Shelley Barry*

Four black shoes dancing
back, forth, side, twirl
slide,
stepping in between.
Black shoes of suede and patent leather
got a vibe going down
on a wooden floor in Woodstock –
some party in a cul-de-sac.

Her feet are bigger than mine
maybe a size 9,
she does her laces neatly,
she's together.
Is that what appeals?
Her black shoes
rhyming with yours.

It's just a dance, just a dance
you say,
but I check those black shoes
stepping into lust!

A cockroach cruises by
nervous.
I watch your shoes flirt.
My heart?
A battered ball
between kickin' feet.

I refuse to look up to your faces.
The black shoes have confirmed
You're just another bastard.

# Cover Me, Cover Me
*Zanele Dolly Simelane*

Cover me, cover me . . . Cover me
For I am born butt naked into this world
Cover me for I sip all the turmoil, ludicrous,
Injustices the pure white milk from grieving
Feminist, slave, liberal, victimised and oppressed
Indoni yamanzi . . . that's my mother.

Cover me, cover me, and cover me
For I am the toddler of a boy, playboy, rapist, suppressor,
Freedom fighter, hero, trendsetter, activist, communist
uMnumzane that is my father.

Cover me, cover me, and cover me
For I am the child of religion, cult, custom, ethics,
Gangsters, umagalobha, Afro-jazz, kwaito, house
Lesoke yisigodi sangakithi.

Cover me, cover me, and cover me
For I am the youth of dreadlocks, promiscuity, democracy,
Z3, rights, globalisation, abuse, violence, second economy,
Interfaith, renaissance and bulimia
That is my Society.

Cover me, cover me, and cover me
With petals of wisdom, for . . .
 I come butt naked into this world.

# Between These Thighs

*Looks Matoto*

(inspired by Sarah Jones)

between these i am a complete man
between these thighs an equal woman
i am
between these thighs i can impregnate
and between these thighs i can be
impregnated
oh between these thighs
between these thighs i am not disabled
i see you look at me with scorn
for you once wondered when you
saw a disabled woman pregnant
in a wheelchair
how is that possible
it is time for you to know
between these thighs if you touch me
passionately
something happens between these thighs
a romantic kiss triggers something
between these thighs
between these thighs oh my dear between

these thighs
between these thighs my capability
can match yours and even surpass
oh between these thighs
and still my capability is not limited
between these thighs
nor shall your yardstick measure me
between these thighs
maybe to you it's revelation time
maybe you say alas somebody cry
blasphemy
do you consider this poem a seduction
meant to lure you to a warm place
between these thighs
i just want to deliver to your knowledge
your happiness can be fulfilled
between these thighs
lasting relations have been created
between these thighs
broken hearts have been mended
between these thighs
those who have passed through these thighs
still tell the story about these thighs
treat them with respect
condomise between these thighs.

# Dear Lulu
## *Mlungisi Khumalo*

I dreamt of you last night . . .

The bird that was perched on my balcony
So sweet and so tranquil
Teasing me and hurting me and healing me,
Made me smile and cry and long for a perfumed whisper

How I prayed it would wait for my touch
Have trust in man just this once

Dear sweet little thing
How deep in love I am
My heart envies the humming leaves below
For they soon will embrace and caress you . . .

My hand reaches out with a shiver
A fear of rejection and despair
Won't you be my love
And kiss just a tip of my finger?

The palm of my hand is itching
Calling for dusk to fall

Forgive the insanity of my crooked mind
I doubt if I'll ever be cured

I'll dream of you tonight . . .

'A Different Corner' – Musa Zulu

# These Wheels of Steel
*Musa Zulu*

(from *The Language Of Me*)

I have at times during the past days wondered
What and where my life would be today
Had this tragedy of disability not met me
Leaving me confined to these wheels of steel

Maybe I would be walking up and down
Running around kicking balls with the boys
Maybe I would be jumping up high
To the beat of a song and its pounding drums
Maybe I would be climbing mountains
And scaling the walls to unexplored heights

Or maybe I would be dead . . .

Then I start to ponder and I discover
That on these wheels of steel I do move up and down
Sitting around and talking about the stories of peace and love
Doing things that lovers do – the things that you and I do
On these wheels of steel I still do jump up and down
Happy with the memories of having been a boy and now a man
I still dance to the songs and move with the beat and the drum

In my mind and life climbing mountains and scaling the walls
Exploring each height with every opportunity given

Yes, I have often wondered
When I sit down alone to think in quiet
Whether at all I do still wish for those maybe's
And deep in my mind, body and soul I feel it
– Oh yes and this I do believe! –
That I really don't have any reason to regret
For all that I have ever wished for myself to be
Today I am
And every night before I fall asleep
I know I am glad to be alive
And about that – there is no maybe . . .

# Let Me Be Me
*Lungile Myeni*

(from *Let Me Be Me*)

I am a runner, a racer.
I know paining muscles
And the pleasure of winning.
When I stumble or fall,
I stand upright
With happiness in my heart
For I have learnt how not to fall.

In dark days
When the storm is blowing,
When there is no sunshine,
I pray with a song in my heart.

For each storm I face,
Each blow I get
Is a step to take me higher.

There is no magic, no trick
That can move me to the right or left.
For I have learnt to be me.

In everything I do or think,
I say, let me be me,
Not somebody else.
Oh please! Let me be me.

# Self-realisation

*Shelley Barry*

We pull toward ourselves
In an endless grappling
Understanding never quite comes
Or comes in parts –
Fractions of the whole
That define

Only when the sun
Lies full on your mouth
Can you speak of the inside
Where something silent
Always resides
Tugging you
From periphery
To centre.

# Thisability
*Musa Zulu*

(from *The Language Of Me*)

SINCE MY ACCIDENT, I have been presented with a lot of opportunities to share my story publicly, appearing in various arenas to talk and raise awareness around disability and its needs. It is my strong belief that many of these needs *can* be met by any society that heeds the inner voice of compassion and commits itself to this end. This entails persuading communities, government and business institutions to work together to assist with the social re-integration and economic upliftment of people with disabilities. There is still so much work to be done in this area – research on disability needs and location, awareness campaigns, improved social security and employment opportunities, development of adequate building infrastructure and transport systems and, last but not least, the implementation of counselling and rehabilitation systems geared to assist disabled people with their holistic re-integration into our society.

★ ★ ★

Experiences change us; our way of being and our identity, our views about life and our sense of purpose, the language we use to express what we are as well as the story we have to tell to the world. Tragedies take away from us, but they also present us with new opportunities and abilities. My life altered forever on 20 April 1995. Along with the other changes it brought, the car crash forced me to reassess the way I viewed both myself and life in general. It made me grateful to be alive and presented me with the opportunity to be acquainted with my real purpose on this Earth. It forced me to write a different life story from the one of my early ambitions, allowed me to rediscover that I am an integral part of the human family, and not just an independent and self-serving individual. Up until the moment of the crash, I had lived a charmed life, one that lacked for nothing and was fortunate in every way. It was a life almost completely free of pain and restrictions. But life is not only about ourselves and our personal ambitions; it is about the humanity we share with others, and it is in service to that bond that we rediscover and heal ourselves. Disability has opened my eyes not only to the pain of others, but to my own internal prejudices towards the disabled, conditioned into me by the society I live in. My sole ambition now is to be an instrument of change, to use my experiences and talents in service of the struggle for the emancipation and dignity of all disabled South Africans. It is my burning wish to reach out to as many in need as possible, in the hope that my story will inspire others to find their own happy endings to the personal dramas of pain and trauma that hold them prisoner. As much as I believe that government and business have a crucial role to play in helping to elevate the status of disabled people in our society, I also feel strongly that, as with all struggles, it is those who are directly affected who need to take responsibility for leading their own march towards freedom, empowerment and visibility. This is how I choose to contribute towards the struggle for the recognition of people with disabilities – by writing a book and talking about my life, tracing the ups and downs that came with my experiences – and celebrating my changes as a sign of rebirth, not a mark of death.

★ ★ ★

The first words that my father spoke to me all those years ago when he saw me lying crushed and broken on that cold hospital bed were: 'All things happen for a purpose.' I did not know what he meant then. But today, many years after the crash, I understand. It has taken me a long time to come to terms with what happened to me, but I can genuinely say that I am now happy and at peace with the fact that I have found a home in disability. There are still times when I ask myself if this had to happen to me at all. But I know that it did. It was God's Will, part of His Master Plan, and thus an episode in the story of my life that had to come to pass. During my time in hospital, one of my visitors was a young disabled street-kid called Joseph, whom I had befriended during my visits to the city centre. He was a boy of fiercely independent spirit, who used to wheel himself about on a skateboard. After he saw me in hospital, his words to my father were: 'I am happy that this one has been disabled. We need someone like this.' At the time, his words seemed very harsh to me. But I have come to see them in a different light, and to realise that my call to disability was a call to arms in service of a cause that badly needs its champions. Through it, so much has been unveiled to my eyes. I have come to appreciate the power of prayer and have been drawn closer to God and the peaceful acceptance of life and whatever it brings. I see myself now as an instrument of God's song – of His beautiful music of love and healing – and I 'sing' His message to the world in every way that I can.

Paralysis has cast a little more magic on me and offered me the chance for a new beginning. I have grown and matured enormously as a result of the accident. There are, of course, still times when I stumble and fall, when I break my head open trying to find answers where none exist. There have also been times when I have slipped off the path and resorted to self-destructive means to escape my prison. Then I have to make a special effort to be positive and patient with myself . . . and focus not on the fall, but on rising again. It's been a long, tough road to healing, filled with its share of setbacks, breakthroughs, challenges and triumphs – but I know that things are going to be okay for me now. I have found acceptance of what happened to me, and this has enabled me to embark on a whole new start.

# About the Editor

**Kobus Moolman** was born in 1964 with spina bifida. He teaches Creative Writing in the Department of English at the University of KwaZulu-Natal in Durban.

He is the author of four collections of poetry, including *Separating the Seas* (University of KwaZulu-Natal Press, 2007) and *Time like Stone* (University of Natal Press, 2000), awarded the Ingrid Jonker Prize for 2001. His illustrated long poem, *Anatomy* (Caversham Press, 2008) won the DALRO prize 2009 for the best poem published in *New Coin* magazine.

He has also published a collection of radio plays, *Blind Voice*s (Botsotso Publishers, 2007) which includes his BBC prize-winner, 'Soldier Boy'. His award-winning stage play, *Full Circle* (Dye Hard Press, 2007), premiered at the National Arts Festival in Grahamstown to critical acclaim and was later produced at the Market Theatre in Johannesburg, the Oval House Theatre in London, and the California State Polytechnic University, Pomona.

Kobus was the founding editor of the KwaZulu-Natal poetry journal, *Fidelities* and as co-ordinator of the Fidelities Poetry Project, he conducted creative-writing workshops and readings for a variety of interest groups, from high school youth to prison inmates. He has twice taken part in the prestigious Poetry Africa Festival in Durban.

# About the Contributors

**Shelley Barry** was born in Port Elizabeth. She became a wheelchair user after being disabled by a shooting in the Cape Town taxi wars of 1996, and has worked extensively as a disability rights activist. In 2003 she was awarded a scholarship from the Ford Foundation to study towards her Masters of Fine Arts in Film at Temple University, USA. Her films have been screened at major festivals and events around the world and have won numerous international awards. She has held positions as the Media Manager in the Office on the Status of Disabled Persons in the Presidency and as the National Parliamentary Policy Co-ordinator for Disabled People South Africa. From 2007 to 2008 she was a Carnegie scholar in residence at the University of the Witwatersrand where she was based as a filmmaker. She runs 'twospinningwheels productions', a film production company.

**Jacqui Edwards** was born in Ixopo in KwaZulu-Natal. She is a painter, craft-maker and poet. She is currently living in a home run by the Pietermaritzburg Mental Health Society.

**Robert Greig** is a writer and drama history lecturer living in Cape Town. He has published three volumes of poetry, *The Rule of Cadence* (University of KwaZulu-Natal Press, 2005); *In the Provinces* (Justified Press, 1991); and *Talking Bull* (Bateleur Press, 1975), which received the Olive Schreiner Prize for poetry. He has twice won the Thomas Pringle Prize for drama criticism. He was born with club feet and deformed ankle bones which were removed soon after birth. He has had approximately 25 operations to his feet, with the effect — if not the intention — of allowing him to dodge standing around at parties and enabling him to boogyboard.

**Jillian Hamilton** was born in Cape Town. She was paralysed in an accident as a child. She now lives on a self-supporting farm in the KwaZulu-Natal Midlands.

**Kevin Dean Hollinshead** was born in 1963 in Rhodesia. In 1986 he did a BSc HDE at the University of Natal, Pietermaritzburg. He was involved in a taxi accident in 1993 which left him severely brain damaged. He is wheelchair bound and has no speech, with only short-term memory. Prior to his accident he was a teacher at Amanzimtoti High, a lecturer at Mangosuthu Technikon and a Technical Training Manager at National Brands. He enjoyed parachute jumping, mountain biking, and running triathlons. He writes poetry and communicates with a laptop Lightwriter.

**Mlungisi Khumalo** contracted polio as a child. He has worked as Project Manager at the Office on the Status of Disabled Persons in The Presidency. A former school teacher, he has also worked as Co-ordinator for Education and Arts and Culture at the South African Federal Council on Disability in Cape Town. As a keen music promoter and artists' manager, he also works with disabled musicians, promoting them in the music industry. He has published poetry and short stories in isiZulu. He is currently working in the Office of the Deputy President in The Presidency.

**Sithembele Africa Lunguza** was born in 1977. He manages the Office on the Status of Disabled Persons with the Eastern Cape Provincial Government. He has a BA degree in Social Sciences from Rhodes University, a postgraduate diploma in International Studies and a certificate in International Conflict Studies from Uppsala University in Sweden. He was diagnosed with epilepsy as a very young child. He is currently completing his MPhil in Disability Studies with the University of Cape Town.

**Mandla Mabila** has a degree in Fine Arts from the University of the Witwatersrand. He is a prominent artist whose works are held in both public and private collections. He works as Regional Co-ordinator for the MAPPP-Seta skills development body in Johannesburg. He is currently completing his dissertation for his Masters degree. He contracted polio at the age of three.

**Mak Manaka** was born in Soweto in 1983. He was disabled after a near fatal accident at the age of twelve. His career as a performance poet has taken him onto international stages where he has performed with Linton Kwesi Johnson and Benjamin Zephaniah, amongst others. He has performed for both President Thabo Mbeki and former president Nelson Mandela. He has published a collection of poetry entitled *If Only* and was nominated for the 2005 Daimler-Chrysler Poet of the Year Award. In 2008 he launched his debut CD entitled *Word Sound Power*.

**Looks Matoto** was born in Port Elizabeth. He contracted polio at the age of five. He has a long and distinguished career as a cultural activist and poet that dates back to the early eighties when he recited his poems at political rallies and funerals. He has been a constant source of inspiration to other writers. He performs regularly at local and international arts festivals.

**Piwe Mkhize** contracted polio at birth. He is an Acting Deputy Manager with the Communication Support Directorate of the KwaZulu-Natal Department of Transport in Pietermaritzburg, specialising in co-ordinating internal and external publications. A budding filmmaker, he is one of the *Echo* community newspaper columnists, as well as a grassroots cultural organiser. He is a Ford Foundation Fellow with the University of KwaZulu-Natal. In 1990, he compiled an anthology of poetry by his late brother, Mlungisi Mkhize, entitled *One Calabash, One Gudu* (Skotaville).

**Sipho Mkhize** was born in Pietermaritzburg. He was active in a range of community organisations during the late eighties and early nineties. He was shot during the notorious Seven Day War in Edendale and lost his right leg. He was later jailed for fifteen years for his involvement in politically motivated acts. His poems have frequently appeared in the KwaZulu-Natal poetry journal, *Fidelities*.

**Zohra Moosa** lives in Durban. She is the first deaf person to qualify in Information Technology without a Sign Language interpreter. She is currently doing a BA degree through UNISA. She works for a shipping company, but would like to become a psychologist for the deaf one day.

**Lungile Myeni** was born in rural Ingwavuma in KwaZulu-Natal. She is partially sighted as a result of cancer. She attended the Open Air School in Durban, where in 2003 she was awarded the Cedric Hilson award for outstanding courage in the face of difficulty and suffering. Her poetry collection, *Let Me Be Me*, was published by umSinsi Press in 2004. She is currently doing her Masters in Clinical Psychology at the University of KwaZulu-Natal. Her dream is to make a difference in the lives of others.

**Motsoakgomo 'Papi' Nkoli** became disabled as a result of a head injury at the age of fifteen. His accident resulted in him becoming a wheelchair user, as well as having epilepsy. He has a Masters degree in Sociology from the University of the Witwatersrand. He is the co-founder of Township

Social History Projects (TOWNSHIP), a company which researches the history of township communities. He is also a member of Disabled People South Africa's Provincial Executive Committee in Gauteng, and of the Council of Africa Institute of South Africa. In his spare time he paints, sketches and writes poetry.

**Giulio Scapin** was born with cerebral palsy. His poems have been published in the KwaZulu-Natal poetry journal, *Fidelities*.

**Zanele Dolly Simelane** was born in Ntuzuma township in Durban. She holds an Honours degree in Drama Studies from the University of KwaZulu-Natal. She was the Project Officer for the Campus HIV/AIDS Support Unit at the same university. She was born with albinism.

**Heinrich Wagner** is from Cape Town and represented South Africa at the World Cup blind cricket in India in 1998, when South Africa secured the cup. In addition, he has crewed on a Cape to Rio racing yacht and is the first blind person to have ridden a bicycle unassisted. His autobiographical script, *Bat Magic*, was launched at the National Arts Festival in Grahamstown in 2003. Heinrich holds the world land speed record for blind driving. He has completed both the Hong Kong and the New York City marathons. In 2005 he started his own company called Visiontree. It focuses on motivational work and corporate entertainment, but also assists disabled people to find fulfilling jobs in the open labour market. He aims to pilot a Boeing 747 from London to South Africa one day.

**Barbara Watt** was paralysed in a shooting accident at the age of three. She has twice represented KwaZulu-Natal in Sport for the Disabled. She lives in Pietermaritzburg, and is the co-ordinator of Disability Connexion at Africa Enterprise, an international Evangelical organisation.

**Musa Zulu** was disabled in a car crash at the age of 23. He is a tireless campaigner for the cause of people with disabilities, and is a well-known motivational speaker. He was the former Director of the KwaZulu-Natal Asiphephe Road Safety campaign. Musa is a writer, poet and artist. His autobiography, *The Language Of Me*, was published by the University of KwaZulu-Natal Press in 2004. *Wheels on the Soul of My Shoes* was published by Nutrend Publishers in 2008. Musa is married to Jay-Jay. They have two daughters, Swazi and Ziyanda.

**William Zulu** was born in Emondlo near Vryheid in 1956. Having contracted spinal TB as an infant, he underwent misplaced corrective surgery to his spine in his late teens which left him paralysed. He studied graphic art at the Rorke's Drift Art and Craft Centre, where he earned widespread acclaim for his striking linocuts. William has exhibited his work in Sweden, Germany and the United States. His autobiography, *Spring Will Come*, was published by the University of KwaZulu-Natal Press in 2005 and was a finalist in the Sunday Times Literary Award 2006. One of his short pieces, 'Echoes of a Distant City' appears in the collection *Durban in a Word* (Penguin, 2008). William is also an isiZulu translator.

# About the Open Air School*

The Open Air School in Durban was founded 89 years ago to cater for learners with physical disabilities. Many of these learners come from very disadvantaged backgrounds and because of the distance of their homes, board at the school hostel.

Despite the extreme physical challenges that pupils face, which often results in them having to miss school for long periods, they continue to achieve at high levels both academically and personally. This is partly due to the unstinting support they receive from the Open Air School staff - from teachers to medical personnel to support staff. The school's motto is 'I can and I will' and its famous 'team spirit' is what helps to instil the confidence for success. In spite of financial constraints and an increase in student numbers, it has maintained its dedication to excellence, achieving 100% matric pass rates in all but one of the past ten years. Two of its matrics have earned top achiever awards from the KZN education department. Learners also excel in the sports arena, with representation in disabled sporting teams at both provincial and international level. A particular source of pride is the fact that two past pupils of the Open Air School were chosen for the South African team that competed with such distinction at the 2008 Paralympic Games in Beijing.

---

* All royalty proceeds from this book will be donated to the bursary fund of the Open Air School to assist with the schooling and board of indigent learners.